A
PERFECT
PRACTICE

A PERFECT PRACTICE

How to establish and
maintain a successful practice in
holistic health and healing

BELINDAGRACE

ROCKPOOL
PUBLISHING

A Rockpool book
PO Box 252, Summer Hill, NSW 2130, Australia
www.rockpoolpublishing.com.au
facebook.com/RockpoolPublishing

First published in 2017

A copy of this publication can be found in the National
Library of Australia.

ISBN 978-1-925429-71-8

Edited by Olatundji Akpo-Sani
Cover by Farrah Careem
Printed and bound in Australia

10 9 8 7 6 5 4 3 2 1

CONTENTS

INTRODUCTION

Every year thousands of talented students graduate from holistic health and complementary medicine colleges all around the world. Many of them will start seeing clients and patients within an existing practice or centre, or set up on their own. Sadly, the challenges of turning their skills and passions into a viable business often means that they struggle for years or discontinue their practice in favour of a more stable job and income, but this does not need to be the case.

'A Perfect Practice' is a straightforward guide that will take you step-by-step through all you need to know about establishing and maintaining a successful practice. It addresses the emotional highs and lows that often confront you when you graduate and leave the support and structure of the learning environment. Packed with real-life examples, it gives you clear suggestions about what to look for in a bricks-and-mortar- and an online practice. It shows you how to

promote your business and how to make money doing what you are passionate about.

Whether you are a brand new counsellor, osteopath, naturopath, massage therapist, reiki practitioner, acupuncturist, chiropractor, astrologer, medium or psychic, you can benefit from the twenty years of the author's experience as a successful practitioner in a variety of mind, body, spirit health and healing fields. And if you have an existing practice and feel that you are not reaching your potential, then this book is also for you.

You have put so much time, energy, effort and money into qualifying as a practitioner, now it's time to turn that into personal fulfilment and professional success.

BelindaGrace is a clairvoyant healer and homoeopath with over twenty years' experience in her field. She is also a popular author and travels the world giving talks, lectures and running extensive workshops. Her books are published in several languages, and she has made numerous TV, radio and magazine appearances in Australia and the USA.

Before becoming a 'success' BelindaGrace made all the mistakes, some of them several times over. She started with nothing more than a diploma and loads of determination. Now she has a thriving practice both online and in person, with clients from every corner of the globe. Many of the graduates from her practitioner training courses have their own successful practices and have particip   BelindaGrace's professional supervision progr

Now, for the   elindaGrace shares the secrets of her professional supervision programs in this book, so that you can start your own practice quickly and with confidence.

CHAPTER ONE

THE WISDOM OF PERSEVERENCE

I am happy to share with you that over the last twenty years I have made all the mistakes, some of them several times over. There are so many things about succeeding and being happy in this line of work that simply aren't obvious. Every few years I would wonder why on earth I hadn't stayed in my high-paying job and just put up with those pressures and stresses because, from a distance, they seemed preferable to the highs and lows of fumbling around and trying to make my business work while getting by on a meagre income.

In starting my own little practice, I often felt like my sole purpose in life was to pay everyone else first: the insurance company, the landlord, the government, the tax department, the professional associations, the printer, the telephone company, the internet provider, the website developer, the mentor … you get my meaning. Even before I saw my first few clients most of these bills had to be paid and they haven't stopped since that very first day.

Then there were the emotional demands of dealing with people's needs and inconsistencies. Working with them to heal their health and feel better about themselves was a delight for me. I enjoyed the actual work, but dealing with phone calls at all hours of the day and night, a growing stream of emails, the no-shows, the late arrivals and the people who claimed they couldn't afford my incredibly low-priced services, were challenges I had not banked on. The luxury of employment in medium-to-large companies had largely shielded me from all of these things. Sure I'd had to endure office politics and meet demanding targets, but as part of a pecking order in a company of any size there is still a level of detachment from the successes and failures of the business and the personalities of the people you have to deal with, which is not present when *you* are the business.

Maybe I am making it sound like it's all about the money. That's not my aim here; my aim is to point out that running your own business from scratch is difficult and much more challenging, on a deeply personal level, than any job. It's my belief that the world would be a very different place if everyone had to run their own business at least once in their lives. And not just run the business, but live only from the proceeds of it.

I took so much for granted when I was employed, from the phone calls I used to make from the office, right through to holiday pay (I thought this was something I was *entitled* to!) and my company car. I can't tell you what a shock it was to receive my first phone bill after leaving the fashion industry, not to mention the costs of running my own vehicle.

On a personal level, I also found the complementary health field very challenging. It was a huge learning curve for me and I had a lot to learn about caring and supporting, without trying to rescue people. To be honest, I was probably playing the role of rescuer for about the first ten years of my practice. Naively, I had just assumed that if someone was willing to spend their time and money coming to see a homoeopath, and then Clairvoyant Healer, they must be the type of person who was willing to take responsibility for their health and their lives. I was shocked to find how needy people could be, and I exacerbated that neediness by believing I had to help them and be available at all times. That was a very hard lesson for me. I still find it ironic that when I am more firm with someone about my boundaries i.e. 'you get 110 per cent from me in the time we have together, then when you walk out that door it's up to you', they have much better outcomes than they did back in the dark ages when I played agony aunt to almost everyone.

It was an emotional, personal, physical, mental and financial rollercoaster as I figured out that other peoples' health and happiness were not my personal responsibility. Once I realised that all I could do was my best, my whole life started to become a great deal more rewarding and enjoyable.

So, was giving up ever really an option? Yes, in my monkey mind it was. We always have options and I believe that if you really want to do it you can reinvent yourself any time you like. It might not be easy, but it's possible. I held down many different part-time jobs during those first ten years, enjoying the relative security and absolute necessity of some dependable income. I did what I had to do to stay afloat, but when I was really honest with myself I knew that I couldn't go back to the fashion industry because it just wasn't my truth. My physical and emotional health had deteriorated so much during my fashion years, and I knew that my body was telling me 'this isn't for you'. Still, I applied for jobs and went for interviews from time to time when it was hard to see the light at the end of the self-employment tunnel.

Now as I look back over the last twenty-five years, I can see that this journey has been the making of me and that there have been far more good times than bad. I've met and worked with some incredible people, and I've designed my own life to incorporate hobbies and other activities I love. Each day my work brings me the joy and satisfaction of working with people who want to shift their energy, raise their vibration and create the best life that they can. I now travel the world promoting the books and card sets I've written and doing readings and seminars in amazing locations and beautiful countries. I have a dedicated following of clients and students worldwide, and most importantly, a wonderful network of friends all around this wonderful planet.

Did I know all of this was going to unfold when I graduated with my homoeopathy diploma over twenty years ago? Of course not! But I have always been willing to dream big. You are reading this book because you want to be happy, healthy, fulfilled, successful and make a positive impact on the world. You are reading this book because you want to save yourself time, find solutions to your dilemmas, find answers to your questions, have moral support and get on with it. You are reading this book because you have a passion and the knowledge that you don't want to, or can no longer fit into, the standard mold of what a normal life is meant to look like. You are reading this book because you are extraordinary and you are willing to dream big too.

For all those things I acknowledge you, and I hope that you will find my offerings, in the form of this book, useful, practical and inspiring.

CHAPTER TWO

GRADUATING IS JUST THE BEGINNING

It may be a difficult pill to swallow, but the truth is that attaining your qualification is sometimes the easiest part of your journey to becoming a holistic health practitioner. Whilst studying is demanding, it can also be a great deal of fun, and there is always support available from your fellow students, the lecturers and the college. Once you leave the security of this structure however, it can be a very different story.

Many graduates fall into an emotional and motivational hole after the excitement and effort of graduating. After fulfilling a dream such as attaining a diploma, you have every right to want to celebrate. So congratulate yourself, feel proud and enjoy the moment. Then get ready for the next big life-changing evolution you will experience as you take what you have learned into the demanding and challenging commercial world.

Maintaining a connection with some of your fellow students after graduation is incredibly important and can provide considerable comfort as you venture out on your own. I can't emphasise this enough. It seems so obvious and yet time and again I counsel clients whose fledgling practices are struggling because they are trying to do it all by themselves. Being part of a community is an amazing resource. When you are establishing a new practice or trying to grow an existing one, you need friends and supporters.

Whilst life is busy and it's easy to drift away from your peers and lecturers after your online or on-campus course ends, it is absolutely vital to your ongoing success and happiness to have a network to stay in touch with. If you haven't finished your studies yet, please make the time to establish a group that meets regularly. I still belong to a couple of alumni groups, and even though I can't attend every gathering I love being invited and kept up to date with their activities. It's so nice to feel a part of something.

If there is already a group available then your participation at some level is important. You will receive much more from it than you ever have to give if you go in with an open mind and a willingness to share experiences and learn from the other participants. Over the years, some of the groups I've been involved with have asked a different member to give a little presentation to the rest of the group each time we meet. So we really had a chance to listen to, and ask questions about, what that person was going through, and what they'd learned. It can also be fun to invite your former lecturers, and people who have already succeeded in your field ahead of you, to come and be guest speakers for your group.

If you have already finished your course and are not connected to any of your fellow students, now is the time to reach out and reconnect. Don't be afraid to contact your most recent lecturers either, as they may be able to reconnect you with other students they are still in touch with. Your educational institution may also be able to help you with this. Simply assuming that you will stay in touch, or that someone else will contact you, is a big mistake. It's very easy for everyone to slip back into their own lives after the course concludes, so you need to be proactive.

When you are willing to reach out and connect you will find that many of your peers feel like you. In this digital age of Facebook, Skype, Zoom and Google Hangouts it's also possible to include people who have moved away from the geographical area, or maintain contact with your peers from an online course. There really is no excuse and 'not having enough time' is the least acceptable one because the very success of your practice may depend upon your involvement.

Some of your lecturers may also offer ongoing, postgraduate support, either formally via the college or as an initiative of their own. For example, the graduates of my five-day intensive courses are able to enroll in my professional supervision program, which gives them affordable access to me for two meetings a month via Skype, for three, six or twelve months, as they choose. I support them in the areas of developing their skills and establishing their business. I focus specifically on whatever the graduate needs the most help with. This can include everything from what fee structure to charge, to proofreading the copy for their brochures and websites before they publish.

But the most valuable aspect of my program is the emotional support. Time and again my graduates tell me how much they look forward to our meetings. Having someone to discuss your anxieties and doubts with is the best way to deal with them, so don't be an island. If none of your lecturers are offering this kind of postgraduate support maybe you could suggest it to them.

I'm a very independent and sometimes stubborn person myself, so believe me, I know how tempting it is to tell yourself that you'd rather do it your way and learn from your own mistakes, but why struggle on your own when you don't have to? I treasure the people who share their advice and expertise with me, and after more than twenty years in my own practice, I am still learning.

So the first thing you do, before you become embroiled in all the practical aspects of setting up your practice, is make sure that you have at least one other person from your course to connect with and a schedule of planned meetings in your diary. Make the meeting locations enjoyable and interesting, but do ensure that everyone can hear each other and that there are not too many distractions. If you are going to connect online then be clear about what platform the meeting will take place on and check that everyone knows how to use it. Last but not least, make sure that everyone is on the same page regarding time, date and venue or platform, so that the maximum number of people will attend. One of my alumni groups uses Facebook to great effect here and a couple of people have willingly taken responsibility for posting the event information and sending out a reminder. It's all so simple, yet it's amazing how easily a basic program like this will fall apart if the fundamentals aren't taken care of.

Your willingness to contribute something to the ongoing organisation and quality of these gatherings will also help you to develop skills that are essential to the success of your practice. So you might as well start now by contributing to this wonderful foundation that can benefit you for many years to come.

CHAPTER THREE

MAKING THE TRANSITION TO BEING SELF-EMPLOYED

Enthusiasm is wonderful and when it comes to making this huge transition you will need it in spades. It is very important to take a balanced approach to transitioning out of student life and/or out of paid work into your own practice. Irrespective of whether you are a student or already working, if you have never run your own business before there are some crucial elements you need to take into account.

As you are unlikely to employ staff at this early stage you will generally fall under the heading of 'self-employed' or 'sole trader'. Working from this position is less costly than leasing commercial premises all on your own or having employees, but you will still have many costs in the process of setting up and maintaining your new business. You will also have all your usual living expenses to pay for. So your transition needs to take into account that the first year or two of being a professional practitioner may actually cost you money.

It can take a few years to find your feet, pick the location you prefer to work from, know how much you can realistically charge (this can vary a great deal between city and rural areas), figure out how to juggle your new venture with the existing demands of your life, and so on. It's best not to overburden yourself in the beginning.

If you are a student graduating straight out of college, I highly recommend that you take a regular job with a regular income, while you develop your practice. Only you can be honest with yourself about your realistic financial needs, so only you can decide what your regular minimum income needs to be. Always make allowances for the expenses in setting up your business when calculating how much you will need to earn to both get started and keep yourself afloat in the first two years. Wherever possible, seek employment that will leave you free on Saturdays because that is the most popular day of the week and you will attract more clients if you are available on Saturdays.

If you are currently employed, the safest way to get started as a practitioner is to make yourself available to clients on Saturdays, whilst keeping your job. Working six days a week can certainly be tiring, but it's a much better strategy than letting your income go at this early stage. As your business starts to develop you may be able to cut your job back to three or four days a week and even add a day or half-day to your practice, if the demand is there.

For me it was a transition of approximately ten years. During my years of study I had been managing a bookstore Monday to Friday, and I set up my first practice a short distance from the store. I saw clients at my home on Saturdays (more about the ups and downs of working from home in coming chapters) and went straight from my job to the centre to see clients outside of usual office hours. In those early days I had plenty of shifts with no bookings at all. So take a good book or your laptop with you and be prepared to while away some hours, remembering that you'll still be paying rent for your room whether you see a paying client or not.

Be cautious but not too cautious when it comes to reducing reliable income in favour of your work. You will need to take some risks, but you don't need to go overboard. In the early days you'll probably bend over backwards to make yourself available for a paying client whenever it's convenient for them, but don't be too accommodating. You need to start educating people about your availability, from the beginning, and stick to your boundaries, within reason. There will always be exceptions, but for the most part, if people can see that you are only available Thursday nights and Saturdays until 2 pm, then they will find a way to see you if they really want to.

Bear in mind that it is also possible to be too cautious when making this transition. Even if you don't have a client every week, it's better to be available every Saturday, for example, than every two weeks or once a month. Your prospective clients will find that much more difficult to keep track of. They will ask themselves, 'now is this the weekend he/she is available or not? I just can't remember'. If you really can't or don't want to be available every week then at least make it very clear on all your publicity material that it's 'The first Saturday of every month' or 'The second and fourth Saturday of every month' and then stick to what you advertise because one of the easiest ways to lose people's interest, in the days before you have built a reputation, is through inconsistency.

When embarking on a new business journey most people do very little or no research into the basics of setting up and running a business. Please don't be one of those people! The peace of mind, both personal and financial, that you will feel from doing some reading, research and asking experienced people for their advice, will save you untold amounts of time and stress in years to come. As with all things in life, especially when establishing a practice, you don't know what you don't know. So sometimes the learning curve is just about learning what questions to ask. So I am glad that you are reading this book because I'm here to help you with that.

Talk to anyone you can in your field, or similar fields, who is doing well and enjoying it. You may need to book an appointment with one of your final year lecturers. Mine charged me his full consultation fee, but it was well worth the opportunity to pick his brain! Most state and federal governments have websites that will provide information for prospective small business owners, and you can go online or to your local library or bookstore to take a look through all the books on establishing a small business in your country. I recommend going to a library or bookstore first, because things aren't always what they seem on internet shopping sites and you don't want to throw your money away on reading what's not appropriate to your situation, so go ahead and browse.

Last but not least, please comb through your local government business websites for links on how to register your business name, how to apply for taxation filing and business numbers and so on. This can feel overwhelming at first, but if you work your way methodically through the website and cross-reference it with what you have read in books, you will soon discover the sequence you need to proceed through. The more you do of this kind of learning before you have your first day in practice, the better and stronger your foundations will be.

When making the transition into earning your own living as a complementary therapist, you will always sleep more soundly if you have a regular income that covers your essential living expenses until you are sure your business is strong enough and consistent enough to support you. Even if it does take ten years before you finally give up part-time work forever, you can stay sane and maintain healthy levels of enthusiasm and joy to share with your clients. Even if all of your friends and family have promised to come for a consultation, I urge you to have a steady income to cover your essentials. Other people will not have the same sense of urgency as you when it comes to booking an appointment, and a few months can easily slip by before that friend comes along for a treatment.

Even if you seriously dislike your job, I encourage you not to throw the baby out with the bathwater. Be grateful for whatever income you can generate while you are getting established, because when you feel financially secure and stable you will pass on those good vibrations to your clients.

Okay, you are off to a good start. You have your network of friends, peers and colleagues to share your journey with and go to for input and advice when you need it. You have a strategy for making your gradual transition from full-time study or employment to a thriving practice whilst maintaining a healthy balance. So what else do you need in this early stage for your business? My suggestion is to keep things simple in the beginning and conserve your cash.

It is not necessary for you to be a member of every professional association that supports your modality, nor is it necessary to attend every meeting or seminar those associations offer. During your first two or three years of business you need to network, listen to the experiences of others and shop around for what will best suit you as your practice evolves. Keeping it simple will save you money and help you to keep your options open while you feel your way into how your practice will develop. Too often I have seen graduates rush out, buy brand new equipment and spend a fortune on memberships and professional seminars only to find that it doesn't bring them any immediate returns or increase their client base. As long as your equipment is clean and safe it doesn't need to be new. So please check your local buy and sell websites and college notice boards for massage tables, office furniture and the like, at affordable prices.

This is the time at which stepping into an existing practice can be hugely advantageous. If you are a newly qualified naturopath for example, perhaps you could seek out a practice that already boasts a fully stocked dispensary. If you are a budding chiropractor then maybe you can team up with an experienced chiropractor in their practice and utilise their expensive, motorised treatment table. As a homoeopath you might want to consider investing in a radionics box so that you can make any remedy you need on demand, rather than trying to stock the thousands of remedies and potencies found in the materia medica.

A little less of 'How can I do this all on my own?' and a little more of 'How can I creatively collaborate and spread costs with others?' will make your life a whole lot easier when you are starting out. Ten years from now, you will be the senior and successful practitioner who can share your infrastructure and expertise with other new practitioners, but for now, you are the one who will benefit from this approach, and you'll compensate the other party by paying your share for whatever you use. It's a win-win situation.

Insurance is a sometimes vexing aspect of our work as complementary therapists. There was a time when I could not find a company that would insure a 'clairvoyant' but the industry has caught up with what is actually happening out there in the real world, and most modalities can get cover now. I'm hesitant to recommend specific companies because I want you to do some of the legwork, shop around and make sure you are happy with whatever cover you buy. At the time of writing, I am a member of the International Institute of Complementary Therapists (IICT), and I have my insurance through them and their association with their insurer. If the IICT seems to offer what you need, at a price you are prepared to pay, then maybe I have saved you some time by mentioning them here, but I just want to make it clear that I am not recommending them as 'the best'. They are simply the organisation I use at this time because I found them professional, easy to communicate with, helpful and reasonably priced. So please shop around and take up public liability and professional indemnity insurance if it feels right for you, if it is a requirement of your profession and/or the locations where you practice and if it offers you the cover you feel you require.

Maintaining your professional accreditation is also very important and most modalities have associations which offer seminars and other events that you can, or must, attend to maintain your qualification. Obviously, this is a great idea because it ensures that you are keeping your skills up to date, and it can reassure your clients and the general public as to your ability and professionalism. In the early years of your practice it's very important to stay on top of this even if your business is slow to develop initially, because it's so much more difficult to catch up if you lag behind the annual requirements. Please make sure you are on the mailing list of the associations and institutions you need to stay in touch with, so that you can be informed of any upcoming events or changes to their points or other accreditation systems.

If you have a selection of seminars or other events that would contribute to your ongoing accreditation, I suggest you attend the ones that will most actively assist in promoting your practice and enhance your business skills as well as the expected focus on your overall proficiency as a practitioner. Of course, if you have the money, time and inclination, I would encourage you to attend as many as possible, but if you need to be selective then it's a good idea to take a businesslike approach so that you will derive the maximum benefit from the time and money you spend.

One more word about equipment and rooms. Please make sure that the environment you practise in is warm and inviting without looking like your lounge room, and it's clean and professional without looking like a surgery. It will depend a lot on which modality you are offering and what type of clients you'd like to attract. Naturally your equipment, furniture and décor needs to be comfortable for you and a reflection of your personality and passions — e.g. I like to have images or figurines of angels or chakras in my treatment rooms. You should consider going easy on things like incense, oil burners and music. All of these things should provide a pleasant background and not overwhelm the space.

As I said earlier in this chapter, as long as your equipment is clean and safe it doesn't need to be new. So be canny with your hard-earned dollars in the early stages and don't tell yourself you have to buy everything new at this stage. You may also be sharing a space with other people who utilise the same room on different days. If this is the case, please make sure you are clear about which items are for general use, which items are exclusively for use by which practitioners and where your storage space will be allocated. Also make sure you are clear on how the room is to be left once your shift or day is finished. It's these seemingly small matters that can cause a lot of ill feeling between practitioners and centre management. Starting out from day one with a respectful awareness of what the other people in the business expect and what you require from them, will make your time there so much more enjoyable.

Finally, a quick word about accounting, bookkeeping and paperwork. It's extremely important to be honest with yourself about your relationship with paperwork. If it is not your forte then please, please, please use an accountant or bookkeeper so you don't get into a mess you can't unravel. It may feel like an unnecessary expense in those early years when your business isn't earning much, but it's an investment and can save you hours of misery and stress later on. For me, word of mouth recommendation has worked best when choosing an accountant, and there are always the franchise organisations like H & R Block.

You can sign up for online accounting platforms like Reckon or Xero, just be sure you are aware of your ongoing financial commitment as their monthly fees can add up. Keeping your receipts, expenses and paperwork in good order is really just another habit that you can cultivate. It's not my forte either, but I just knuckle down and do it every few months. Each time I do it I find that it's never as difficult as I expected.

Now don't laugh, but my system is very rudimentary. I keep all my statements and tax invoices in one envelope, a large yellow envelope for each month. I then track all my incoming and outgoing monies via my credit card statement and bank statements. I also use PayPal for accepting payments and making purchases, and I take the information I need from the monthly statements they supply. Then I write it all out by hand in a ten-column book designed for bookkeeping purposes and hand all that to my accountant. It's neat, simple, I know where I'm at and the accountant can see it's all verified by receipts and invoices.

As my business becomes more international and involves more and more travel, I will transition across to an online system like Reckon, so I can have access to accurate exchange rates and work online wherever I am in the world. In your early years, simply getting into the habit of recording what you spend, keeping receipts and tax invoices in a folder and developing a system, will be a good start. I suggest you make an appointment with a bookkeeper and see it as an investment in your education and business. One hour spent with an expert will save you countless hours of trying to figure it out yourself. They will show you how to keep records, tell you what it is they need to know, set you up with a system that works for you and generally take a load off your mind. As the years pass your relationship with your bookkeeper and/or accountant can be an enjoyable one and can be vital to the financial success of your business.

CHAPTER FOUR

SHOW ME THE MONEY

Would you expect a mechanic to fix your car for nothing, or a solicitor to draw up documents for you for free? Would you go to the doctor and expect them to treat you out of the goodness of their heart? No, I didn't think so. So why is it that so many of the fledgling practitioners I meet have so much trouble charging a reasonable fee for their work? I know I struggled with this part of my practice for years. I undercharged and went 'without' myself, telling myself that I was doing what I loved and that people needed my help. Asking for money made me feel uncomfortable and almost apologetic, in my early years, even though I was charging much less than more experienced practitioners.

My pricing structure was complicated a little more by the fact that I started out as a homoeopath and gradually evolved into working as a clairvoyant healer. Charging for my homoeopathic consultations was simplified by the fact that I could compare myself to what other homoeopaths in Sydney were charging at the time, but as I transitioned more and more into the clairvoyant work I really felt lost and had no idea how to value myself.

If you'd like to know more about my own personal story you can find that information on my website or in my book *You Are Clairvoyant*, but with regard to charging a fee per consultation, this was something I found very challenging. Some people told me that they had seen clairvoyants in the United States who charged $300 an hour. Other people suggested that it wasn't spiritual to earn money from such work and I should do it for free. I must admit I felt that way for a time, perhaps because it felt easier to me to have no fee, or because I wanted to be seen as a good and giving person. The reality was and is, however, that as a clairvoyant healer my cost of living was and is, the same as everyone else's. Food, transport, housing and clothing were not coming to me for free, and if I wanted to survive in my practice I had to charge enough to cover my costs and live some too!

Years later, on the final day of one of my five-day residential courses, one student really lost her temper about this topic. She was a hairdresser and understood all the costs and demands of running her own salon, but she became quite indignant with me and the other students as we discussed what we might charge for our work. She declared that 'We are working with universal energy and light, and we should not charge money for that! We should give our time for free!' There was a real sense from her also that somehow we were a bit above 'ordinary' people because this was a 'spiritual' modality.

We all listened, and I could feel the anxiety rising throughout the group. As usual, in challenging situations like this, I don't rely on my own opinions so much as I open up to what my guidance has to say. On the face of it, this student appeared to be attacking me, but in reality she was just afraid of what people would think of her. It was her fear that was doing the talking. So I asked her the same questions I asked you at the beginning of the chapter, and that's where her sense of doing something superior to a trade or job became more obvious.

I replied by saying that no matter what job someone is doing or what task they are performing, when they do it with love, with a positive intention, offering good service and a quality result, then they are also working with universal energy and light! We are not doing something better or more important than them, we are just doing what we do and we deserve remuneration just as much as any person who has gone to the time, trouble and expense of developing certain skills. This student looked a little dumbfounded, and I could see that she didn't like being compared with trades people and other professionals. The fact is, when your car won't start or a tap in your kitchen bursts and spews water all over your floors, you will feel amazing gratitude for the skill and speed of the person who gets that repaired for you with accuracy and integrity.

So, whether you are a massage therapist, counsellor, naturopath, acupuncturist, reflexologist, physiotherapist, Bowen therapist, psychic or clairvoyant, you are working with universal energy and light and sharing your version of it, your gift, with the world. If you don't charge a reasonable fee for your work, you may soon go out of business and then you won't be able to share that good energy with anyone.

In order for you to give genuinely from the heart and feel happy and balanced in your own life, you need to, and are entitled to, earn a decent living. I use the word 'entitled' here advisedly. Please understand that I don't believe that anyone is just entitled to anything. I believe we earn our way in the world. All people are entitled to the fundamentals such as respect and freedom of speech. The entitlement I am referring to here is in relation to the time, effort, energy and commitment you have put, and continue to put, into developing, refining and sharing your skills.

It is always important to gauge what established practitioners are charging in your area. You will probably need to charge in line with the local 'going rate' in your city or region. Some natural therapy and professional centres will insist that you charge within a certain range. This usually works well because they know their market, so if you are comfortable with that it's a good place to begin. If the centre you are renting a room in doesn't want to guide you on price, my general rule of thumb is this: in cities such as Sydney or Los Angeles where room rates are usually quite high – at time of writing around US$100 or AUS$130 for a half-day shift, the fee you charge for one consultation should cover the cost of that half day.

In regional and rural areas where room rental fees are usually much lower, the fee for one consultation will be lower but should still come closer to covering a full day's rental. If you cannot cover the cost of half a day, say 9 am to 2 pm or 2 pm to 7 pm, with the fee from one client, then you are either paying too much for the room or not charging enough. You need to allow some leeway in your first year or two of practice while you are still charging a lower fee. So maybe you won't quite make the rent from one client for that short period of time, but in the longer term you need to aim for the equation above. Otherwise, you'll be working just to pay everyone else.

Working from an established centre can also take the awkwardness out of accepting payments. A centre with a full-time receptionist will usually charge more for room rental, but I prefer this scenario because, not only do they book my appointments, but they take the payments as well. These days I am very comfortable with the fees I charge, so the advantage of a receptionist, for me, is the time I save. If the centre you practise in does not employ a receptionist, there should at least be a desk or counter that you can stand behind when accepting your payment. It seems like a small thing, but there is a definite shift in the dynamic between you and your client when you 'change hats' and step around behind that desk.

If you are working from home or in a room with no other facilities, the digital age offers you some interesting options. In these situations you will most likely take your own bookings, so when you confirm the appointment by email or phone you can ask for the payment then, either verbally or by sending them an invoice. This system of emailing the client an invoice works extremely well for me when I am seeing clients at home. I confirm the time and date of their appointment and list the methods of payment I can accept. More often than not the client will make payment by electronic payment into my bank account or will request a PayPal invoice. When it comes to accepting payments worldwide, I have found PayPal invaluable as their invoicing gives the client the option of paying from their PayPal account or by credit card. Setting up a merchant facility with PayPal is free, which is a lot more than can be said for trying to do the same directly with a credit card company. I also have the PayPal Here app on my phone so I can accept credit card payments wherever I can access the internet.

There are several systems like this available worldwide, so shopping around is always a good idea.

PayPal's fees sometimes seem a little expensive, so I do keep my ears open for other systems and companies. In the USA many small-business people use Cube and more recently I have been introduced to TransferWise, which has been a wonderful find for low-cost money transfers to bank accounts in other countries, at a good exchange rate. Whichever way you do it, I highly recommend that you set yourself up to accept credit cards. It will bring you business, and paying a small fee to the service provider is much more preferable than losing a booking because a client hasn't got the ready cash.

CHAPTER FIVE

LOCATION, LOCATION, LOCATION

One of the most interesting aspects of being a complementary health practitioner is the freedom you can experience when selecting your workplace. Working from home is an obvious first step for a lot of fledgling practitioners because it's a relatively low-cost way to begin. If you are a bit like me, you were probably already seeing the occasional client at home before completing your studies, and sharing your skills with family and friends. If you aren't in your final year yet or haven't tried this, it can be a great way to learn the art of making appointments and preparing a workable space.

It must be said, however, that for most people, working from home will also come with certain limitations. Some of which may even prove to be obstacles to your success. The location you live in will play a major part in whether or not people will be willing or able to come to you. It's as simple as that. No matter how wonderful your skills or how beautiful your rooms, if you live in a distant suburb of a huge city or in an out-of-the-way country town then people will be far less likely to come to your home. It's important not to pretend otherwise.

Working from home can also raise other issues, especially if you live with other people or if your neighbours might be affected. A few years ago I knew a woman who started a yoga studio and massage business out of her home in a residential street of a small town. Someone told her she didn't need council approval for this enterprise, so she just went ahead with her plans. Well, her neighbours soon had enough of four or five cars parking out in their street several times a week for the yoga classes and the council came in and shut her down. Not only did she lose a great deal of money, it was embarrassing, stressful and not good for her reputation.

The message here is not to be naïve about the impact your activities could have on the people around you, or your enthusiasm could soon be dampened by their displeasure, even if they seemed supportive in the beginning. A 'try it and see' approach is best when working from home because in most cases a home is first and foremost a home, and this will prove to be important for you as well, during the times you aren't working.

A word here too on insurance. It's a good idea to look into public liability insurance if you have people

TITLE: A perfect practice : how to estab
BARCODE: 31812056681191
DUE DATE: 11-25-19

TITLE: Dual transformation : how to repo
BARCODE: 31812053968310
DUE DATE: 11-25-19

TITLE: I can't make this up : life lesso
BARCODE: 31812054223038
DUE DATE: 11-08-19

TITLE: Every landlord's guide to finding
BARCODE: 31812052173540
DUE DATE: 11-25-19

TITLE: Perfect is boring : 10 things my
BARCODE: 31812056042097
DUE DATE: 11-25-19

coming to your home for consultations because if someone stumbles and falls in your garden or your massage table gives way, you could be held liable. These days the home office is a very common thing and being able to do your emails and update your website in your pajamas can seem wonderful after years of commuting, so just be sure that you are doing what's necessary to protect yourself professionally and personally.

Take time to think through the logistics of seeing clients at home and the impact it will have on that very important and sacred space. Personally, I prefer to have my consulting room set-up closest to my front or rear door so the client doesn't have to walk through my entire house, partly because I don't want to have to clean the whole house every time someone comes around! Seriously though, my private space is important to me, and I don't want my entire home to feel like work. Are you going to offer your client water or a cup of tea? Is the space comfortably cooled and heated? Many clients will need to go to the bathroom before or after their consultation, so what is the access to the nearest bathroom like? Have you got children at home, a partner working shifts or neighbours who are finicky about parking? None of these things need be a problem ever. It's all about communication with a bit of anticipation and plenty of awareness about the impact you and your business may have.

Over the years I have found it to be true, both for me and for most of my graduates, that it's not only necessary but also hugely beneficial to make that leap into a professional centre. Whilst working from home some days can still be a great option and save you some money on professional rent, I have found nothing can replace the exposure you receive when working in a busy practice surrounded by other busy practitioners. It's inspiring and it's a buzz! It's also good for your bottom line because if the centre is well run, supportive and populated with positive practitioners, you will benefit from direct and incidental referrals, and your client base will grow so much more quickly than if you only work from home. I have seen this happen time and time again,

Obviously, the complementary health centre is likely to be in a much more commercial location with plenty of passing foot traffic (certainly more than outside your home!), and the cost of paying your room rental will in part be compensated by what you will learn and the support you can receive from this professional environment. I'll go into more depth later in the book about succeeding in an established practice, but for now I'd like you to consider a healthy balance. Maybe you don't intend to see clients at home at all, which is sometimes another great option. You can still write your emails and update your website at home with the cat on your lap, if you like, and leave your professional life completely in a professional location.

I have always found that a blend of both works best for me. I enjoy, and my clients appreciate, the flexibility that seeing clients at home can offer, and I always look forward to my days at the professional centres I work in, both here in Australia and around the world. I love the support of a receptionist taking bookings for me and dealing with the repetitive tasks, like giving directions. I love the camaraderie of being around other practitioners from many disciplines and backgrounds. I love the fact that, for a relatively small fee, someone else is providing me with all the infrastructure of their business premises, because that is a responsibility that I don't want.

In the early days of my practice, I was just grateful to have a reason to get out of the house, which was so important for my own mental and emotional health.

In terms of the location of the professional centre, I believe it must be practical for you. If it's going to take you two hours to drive there this will severely diminish your chances of opportunities, like a client walking in without a booking to see who's available. If it's too close to home it might mean that too many of your clients are people that you bump into in the neighbourhood. This may or may not bother you, but it's worth thinking about. Put simply, I have usually been guided via recommendations, word of mouth and good old common sense when choosing a centre in which I'd like to work.

If I like the location, enjoy being there, the owner/ staff are friendly and helpful, their website and/or Facebook page looks good, they answer the phone/ return my call promptly, the other practitioners seem busy and happy, a friend or client has spoken well of it and so on, then that spells success and joy for me. It's also a great idea to sign up for newsletters and 'like' the Facebook pages of centres you may wish to work from one day. That way you can have a regular insight into what is happening in that practice.

So in summary, my recommendation is that you begin by working from home if that is manageable, and build up a little client base. It doesn't have to be enormous, but this will help you when you start applying to professional centres to rent their rooms. Then, start shopping around until you find one or two centres you like the look and feel of, in a location that is appealing and practical for you. Make plans to start small at the centre whilst keeping your home-based clients happy. In this way you can compare both experiences and learn more about what each has to offer. It can be very difficult to run a successful practice solely from home. Some people manage it and some go back to it after years in a professional complementary health centre, and for most of us a combination of the two can work extremely well.

CHAPTER SIX

LIFE IN A BUBBLE

Have you ever wondered why so many self-employed people take their laptops and smartphones to the local café? It's one of the many things I love about travelling in the USA, you can always find a café with great Wi-Fi. Meaning that a sole trader and constant traveller like myself can enjoy a coffee, catch up on emails and mix with other members of the human race all at the same time. Life as a practitioner can be rather isolating at times and it's vital to know how to address this.

Sadly there are many businesses here in Australia that haven't yet caught on to the fact that good Wi-Fi, and a spare power socket or three for recharging mobile devices, is great for business. In the region I live in I'm still barked at sometimes by irate café managers when they find I've plugged in, or where customers still have to ask for a Wi-Fi code or password in order to access it.

Compare this to 'Tom's', down on funky Abbot Kinney Boulevard, near Venice Beach in Los Angeles, for example, where the Wi-Fi is super fast and every table has at least one power outlet practically begging you to use it. There is a great vibe, and I get my work done while waiting for a friend, chatting with someone at another table and yes, actually spending some money on coffee and food too. It's fun and it's a win-win for everyone.

Why am I seemingly having a rant about the availability of Wi-Fi? Because the café has become the new office, and for practitioners like us they are heaven sent. Even if you do work in a professional centre a day or two a week, cabin fever is always lurking in the background. Working from home has many advantages, but it's important to be aware that you need to get out of the house on a regular basis as well. Your mental and emotional health could depend upon it.

If you have never done it before, taking your laptop to a café and sitting on your own with your latté might feel a bit odd because you normally go to a café with your friends right? That's great too; social times at your favourite eatery are national pastimes in most of the countries I travel in, but they can also be wonderful workplaces. Keep an eye out for places that look inviting, have good lighting, power outlets that you are welcome to use and music that isn't overpowering. It will probably already be full of small-business owners like you, so go join that club!

You may also find that you have in your area, commercial communal workspaces that cater specifically to self-employed and small-business people. For a small user-pays, or membership, fee you'll have access to great internet, other office equipment such as a photocopier, desk space, meeting rooms and information about small business education, events and groups that meet regularly at that location. At the time of writing, I can recommend 'Blue Bottle Coffee' on University Ave in Palo Alto, California and 'StartInno Co-working and Innovation Hub', Byron Bay, NSW, Australia, or just check your favourite search engine for co-working hubs in your area. Art galleries often have gorgeous cafés too; I happened upon a real gem in Bath in England at the Holburne Museum. So be creative and discover locations that are good for your soul.

Having a reason to get out of your track pants and head outside is important for everyone, but when you are a practitioner in the complementary health field you definitely need to keep yourself happy and feeling supported. I spoke about this from a different angle in Chapter Two, the need to stay connected with your peers and other support groups, but here I am talking more about your day-to-day life and how easy it is to become isolated in a short space of time.

When you find yourself no longer working in the office or shop, no longer having someone to go to lunch with and no longer involved in those work-related social events, life can suddenly become very lonely. During the honeymoon period, you will marvel at the freedom of not having to be at work by a certain time, love the fact you don't need to commute, revel in the freedom of being able to do a load of washing while writing up your latest newsletter, and enjoy having your own space and pace for a change. Then the reality starts to set in and you realise, for most of us anyway, that there is no one else there to talk to until your children come home from school and/or your partner comes home from work. If you live alone, this chapter is even more crucial. So it pays to get into some healthy habits from the start.

As a complementary health practitioner you will be exposed to peoples' problems, needs, heavy emotions, health challenges and worries. During a one-hour massage your client may be half asleep and hardly say a word, or may be full of aches and pains. As a naturopath you may be faced with the chronic illness or pain your patient has been suffering, and they are looking to you to make things better. Or as a clairvoyant, psychic or medium you may be faced with a client's desperate questions about when they will find true love or how their deceased loved one is doing on the other side. All of the above are needs, and whilst you know that it's not your job to rescue your client or make everything better for them, you are a caring, sensitive human being, and working with people in need can be extremely demanding.

You might tell yourself 'I don't feel alone when I am working from home. I have clients coming here for treatments, and I speak with other clients by phone and Skype. I'm always talking with people.' If you want to believe this then try looking at it from another perspective. Your clients are probably very nice people, but they are not your friends. They are there, in consultation with you because they need, want and expect something from you. During your time with them you are in the role of professional, to get a certain job done. You are supporting *them*, not the other way around. So yes, even though you are interacting with people through your work, it is vastly different from the convivial atmosphere of a local café or hub, and catching up with your peers and friends.

You may well form actual friendships with some of your clients over time, but that is not the aim of your practice. The aim of your practice, from the clients' point of view, is to deliver on your promise so that they walk away feeling better and more optimistic. Your job is to listen, respond and produce results. So to keep yourself in good shape it's important to have a worthwhile, enjoyable reason to leave home most days and connect with other people. You deserve it, and you owe it to yourself and your clients.

A note on fitness. Because most modalities require the practitioner to be sitting for long periods of time in a consultation room and at the computer, it's a great idea to make fitness a regular part of your personal happiness program. For myself, I keep up a lovely weekly mix of beach walks and yoga classes in the mornings and Salsa and Tango classes a couple of evenings a week. I love Latin dancing, and these activities keep me fit, social, and get me out of my chair. Because they are morning and evening, I still have time to go work at a café or gallery during the day if I want. So enjoy!

CHAPTER SEVEN

THE EARLY DAYS

When you are a fledgling practitioner, attracting clients is one of the most daunting aspects of your business. Most people aren't accustomed to, or comfortable with, 'promoting themselves' or what they do. In fact gifted, caring and intuitive people are often notoriously poor at owning their talents and worth. So the delusions, that people will come to you when they are ready, that it's all just word of mouth or that you simply aren't good enough yet, are very tempting to hide behind.

The first two delusions are actually correct from a different perspective. Of course, you shouldn't try to convince people to come and see you, and yes, word of mouth can have a very powerful impact on your client numbers. In the early days you need to find ways to encourage potential clients to take you seriously in order to generate that word of mouth, though. The third delusion can be a difficult and very personal one, but the simplest way to address it is to practise, practise, practise!

The following approach worked extremely well for me in my early days and continues to work well for my graduates. It's the simple act of offering your work for free for a limited time and/or number of visits. No doubt your family and friends have already shown some interest in what you are studying, so it's a natural progression to offer them a free consultation or two. When you are close to graduation, or have already graduated, this process takes on a much greater significance when you put a clear limit on how much free treatment you are willing to offer.

Placing a clear limit on the availability of your free consultations signals to the world that you are becoming a professional and intend to value yourself as such. It also creates a sense of urgency and motivates people to come and see you before your offer expires, which is exactly what you want. This system also creates boundaries that are very important for you to master in your professional practice, and last but not least it's a subtler form of promotion. Even though you aren't professional yet and you're not charging a fee, your happy clients will tell their families and friends about their experience. Your fellow students can also provide a ready group of people with which to practise your skills. So remember to share what you're learning with them and suggest that they refer some of their family and friends to you, and vice versa.

You need to be clear on what you are going to offer and for how long. So here is a simple example. One of my graduates from the USA completed the five-day course in March and set a goal of going professional from the 4th of July weekend onwards. Naturally, her friends and family were excited for her and knew that she was travelling to Australia especially to attend my course. So she harnessed their excitement and kept them up to date via Facebook, during the course. Then she announced that on her return to the USA she would be offering clairvoyant healing sessions until the 4th of July for free, with a maximum of three free visits per person. She intended to offer these sessions from home, but a business owner in her town saw her posts and suggested she might like to hire a room at her practice. So before she even left Australia, my student already had a professional location to work from if she wished.

She maintained the parameters of her offer and was busy beyond all her hopes and dreams. She now has some regular paying clients, works from those professional rooms on a casual basis (no commitment to a fixed rent) and is even beginning to offer small group events, such as a monthly meditation circle complete with guest presenters.

If you are very shy or just don't feel confident in your abilities yet, it's totally fine to take a much slower approach. Another of my graduates was shy, very soft spoken and worked in the IT field. All that, combined with the fact that she had only moved to Australia a few years earlier, meant that she didn't have family nearby, nor did she know many people who were interested in holistic therapies of any kind. She felt stuck.

This graduate was much more comfortable practising only with other students and gradually, with my encouragement, she reached out to them via our alumni group Facebook page. She offered to visit other students at their homes and invited them to hers, establishing some great connections with students from previous courses. Many wonderful things evolved from her willingness to connect with the other students. Not least of which was the realisation that she wasn't the only one who was nervous about practising with people outside the group!

For me the stand-out benefits for her have been the development of her confidence and abilities, increasing her group of friends, learning from the more experienced graduates *and* the fact that one of my graduates who has been seeing his own clients now for several years, has taken her under his wing and is mentoring her. They live near each other and meet up in person, regularly.

If your course is of a few years duration, you may well have a student clinic as part of your final year, which will give you much valuable experience. It's wonderful to have your professor or supervisor there to prompt you if you get stuck, but there will always come that day when it's just you and your client in the room, with no one else there to help you. So practising with volunteers is valuable on so many levels. Obviously, not all of the people who come along for a free treatment will become paying clients. There will always be people who come along only when they don't have to pay, but even they are a blessing for you, because they are helping you to develop confidence and expertise.

Another great way to build a client base in the early days of your practice is to offer your services at festivals and other big public events. You need to think carefully about the context. For example, if you are a massage therapist you probably won't attract the right people for your ongoing business if you set up a stand at a boat or car show. So make sure that the event is something you can reasonably align yourself with. For instance I avoided events where a lot of alcohol was going to be consumed. That was my personal choice, but if you feel comfortable at a big music festival or similar, that's up to you.

The types of events that worked well for me, and continue to work well for my graduates, are mind body spirit festivals, health and wellbeing festivals, yoga festivals, fitness expos and fundraisers for worthwhile causes. I used to love doing readings at fundraising events because, naturally, I donated some of my earnings to the cause and then everyone was happy. At all of these events I made sure I had plenty of brochures and business cards to hand out. Many people weren't in the right frame of mind to have a reading at the event, but I had plenty of follow-up business afterwards. Your regular local craft or wholefood markets are also worth looking into. They can be a great way of tapping into your local community and some market organisers are happy with casual stall holding, which may work better for you if you're not sure about committing to a weekly or monthly stand.

Last but not least, please don't overlook the humble local notice board. Many libraries, stores, university and college common rooms, community centres and clubs still have them, and they can be worth their weight in gold. Always make sure that your poster is clear, to the point and easy to read. Always have tear-off tabs with your name and whatever contact you choose to provide, so that interested people can tear off the little tab, pop it in their wallet and call or email you later. Don't expect people to do the work for you; make it easy for them to take your contact details away, and be sure to check your notice boards regularly to refresh your posters when all the tabs have been taken.

In other chapters we'll talk about social media and promotion through digital channels, but all of the above are still effective, even in this digital age, and can put a much more human face to your offerings.

They are an effective and inexpensive way to promote yourself, while you are gaining the experience you will need once you are a qualified practitioner. It is also helping you to create the foundations of a loyal and growing client base.

CHAPTER EIGHT

BUSINESS CARDS AND BROCHURES

Most of us were not born with an instinctive knowledge of how to promote and market ourselves, so producing an effective range of promotional materials can mean there is a lot to learn. I have found it to be both challenging and fun. There is so much to learn and you won't know how to do it all in the beginning, so keeping it simple is paramount.

When you are seeking out a service, what information are you looking for? Think about that for a while and then relate it to what your potential clients will want to know about you and your services. Business cards, brochures and flyers come in all shapes and sizes. Some of them are bristling with information and some are laconic. Some use colourful images and others are text only. There is a great deal of variety within these mediums because they are an expression of the personality of the practitioner and the image the practitioner is trying to project. Your promotional materials are your ambassadors, and they can pass before many pairs of eyes and through many pairs of hands.

Brochures and flyers — Personally I am still a big fan of brochures and flyers and not much of a fan of business cards. Why? Because when someone gives me their business card I usually lose it or it winds up at the bottom of my handbag. A brochure works better for me, especially if it is printed on attractive stock, because if done well it feels nice to hold as well as looking good. A stock, the paper or card that your item is printed on, with a bit of substance like 120 gsm feels a lot more professional than standard 80 gsm stock, which is the weight of common photocopying paper.

There are numerous things you will want to consider, such as matte or semi-gloss, full colour or black printed on coloured stock. So look around you and collect flyers and brochures that appeal to you. Collect some images that you might like to use. At time of writing, there are some useful websites that provide good quality, royalty free images such as www.pixabay.com and www.freeimages.co.uk, but be sure to read their terms of service first, or step up to affordable images from sites like www.istockphoto.com that don't require you to credit them as the source. You can use your own images too but please make sure they look professional. I see way too many brochures and flyers with blurry or badly lit portrait shots or where the practitioner in question has not made the extra effort with hair and makeup.

As for the content, please keep it simple. What do you want to know when you are shopping around for a practitioner? Keep the description of what you do, clear and to the point. Bullet points provide a good framework and force you to be economical with words, and if you have a diploma or degree make sure you put those letters after your name. Then include the essentials like where to find you (best not to give your home address, suburb is sufficient), when you are available, how to contact you and your fee. Some people think it's clever not to put their fees on their flyer or brochure, but, personally, it has worked well for me. Even in this age of smart phones and Wi-Fi I don't expect my potential clients to do the legwork of having to find out my prices. If they are already reading my brochure, I want to provide them with all the information that will help them to make an appointment.

Brochure size and shape is another interesting matter to consider. For many years now I have been using the DL size and shape for my brochure, and A5 or postcard size for flyers. Typically the A5 flyers are something I use for promoting workshops and events and they are printed on one side only. I usually send a bundle of them to the venue to display on their reception area and notice board, or email them the pdf document and have them bill me for the cost of printing. I use A5 or postcard size for my flyers because that is big enough and most venues don't have unlimited display space. I only go over the A5 size if I know that the flyer will also be used as a poster in a window or similar.

The A5 size can also look really nice when folded in half to form a little booklet and that finished size is great for purses, wallets and pockets. When I first started out and couldn't afford to print full colour DL brochures I used nice quality, coloured paper stock, printed on both sides in black only. Mine was just text and a simple logo, but a quality black and white photo can work too. They were very popular, and I used to receive so many compliments about those brochures. Every now and then I would change the colour of the stock just to keep things interesting or when some of the information changed, such as a price rise. So never underestimate the power of a simple, well presented brochure.

Business cards — Business cards, of course, will hold less information, and back in the days when I still had a business card, I never put my fee on them. I only included that on my brochure. My business cards were always a bit more colourful than average, with a nice image in one corner and printed on a good quality 150 gsm stock. Usually they read something like this —

BelindaGrace Clairvoyant Healing
Clairvoyant Readings

Chakra Balancing
Past Life Release
Angels and Spirit Guides
www.belindagrace.com

That was on the front. Then on the back of the card I would have the name, address, phone number of the professional centre I worked from, my email address and again my website. Have you noticed that something might be missing? That's right, I didn't mention my mobile phone number because I stopped putting that on my business cards years ago. Publicising your mobile phone number is a personal choice. I have always chosen to work in centres that have a full-time receptionist, and for appointments at home I ask clients to email me. I know that this has cost me a few readings over the years, but my privacy is very important to me. I could never get my head around buying a second phone for business use only. So consider your options carefully when putting your mobile phone number out there because many people will not confine their calls to business hours. You can always let it go to message bank of course, but that may nag at you and feel obtrusive. If you can manage two phones and switch your work-related one off at the end of the day, then this may be the system for you.

Many of my graduates will try both a brochure and a business card to find out what works best for them. During their professional supervision program we will discuss wording, layout, design and all other matters relating to creating great marketing material. I encourage them to put a photograph of themselves on the brochure because it engenders trust and helps the client make a connection with you. So please consider using a good quality portrait shot of yourself that is well lit, doesn't have anything distracting in the background and in which you look positive and approachable. I always recommend that you ask a few people for feedback about your photo before going to print because we just don't see ourselves the way other people do!

Quite a few of my graduates have used Vistaprint because they have a wonderful service for free business cards and postcard sized flyers at very economical prices. You design your card or flyer on their website using their templates. They have a small range of artwork available, or you can upload your own images. There is a bit of trial and error with any system like this, but stick with it and you will soon get the hang of it.

Roller banners — Another excellent promotional tool to consider is a pull-up- or roller banner. If you are going to take a stand at your local market or fair, or if you work in a large space or intend to run seminars and workshops, floor-standing- and tabletop banners can look great. You'll feel more professional, and that big blank wall and floor space will be put to good use. Use banners such as these to promote your website, your products and services. If it's all about your product you might not need to include a picture of yourself, but usually it's a good idea to include that too so potential clients can see who they'll be dealing with.

We haven't spoken about logos yet, so now is a good time. Definitely include your logo on your pull-up banners and all your other promotional material such as business cards, brochures and flyers. Regarding the banners, in the USA you can try Staples, Kinko/FedEx or www.popupstand.com. Some of these businesses also offer a design service. In Australia, you can go to Officeworks and Vistaprint, and in the UK I have used www.rollerbannersuk.com. There are plenty of companies producing these nowadays. So you can always shop around.

Logos — So let's go back to logos for a moment; there is no need to feel daunted by the process of having a logo designed. In this amazing internet age we have access to creative talent, worldwide and at great prices. Websites like www.fiverr.com are a great resource when your budget is slim and you'd like to experiment. Many of my graduates had some great logos designed by graphic designers on fiverr.com. The name 'fiverr', yes it has two r's, refers to the fact that most jobs, known as 'gigs', start at US$5, so it's very affordable. You can browse all the available designers, view samples of their work and place an order. Most of the time it's a very quick and satisfying system.

My personal experience with fiverr.com has been largely positive. Overall, I would say that you need to be really clear about what you want and realistic about what's on offer. Choose a designer who is already offering a style that appeals to you, and if you can't find anyone producing the exact look you want then be prepared to upload images for them, to give them some idea of what you want. If I am looking for something different and feeling adventurous, I will sometimes have three or four different designers create a logo for me, just to see what they come up with. By using this approach, I have been pleasantly surprised and saved myself time by not putting all my eggs into just one designer's basket.

Technology — I have had to drag myself out of the computing stone age and learn a lot about how this all works. At time of writing, I am in my mid-fifties and I never had to work with computers before starting out on my own. It can be excruciating! If you don't know a PDF from a TIF, have never created or edited a website before and have no experience designing brochures, then welcome to the human race! You are just like the rest of us, and these are not things you were born knowing, so take it easy on yourself. Get help, ask questions and take a tutorial. You can often find video tutorials on YouTube (there's that technology again) or, as I have done on a couple of occasions, you can pay for private tutoring or attend a class. Community colleges and local tech stores regularly offer classes for the dazed and confused, so invest a little time and money before going down the rabbit hole. It will save you loads of time and might just save your sanity.

CHAPTER NINE

BUILDING YOUR BUSINESS ONLINE

Having your own website is essential these days because it is your 24-hour-a-day global business card and the front door to your business. Your potential clients will use your website as a means of understanding what you do and deciding whether they need your services, so it's very important that your website is clear, effective and to the point.

Most websites have far too much information on them, not enough good images and make it difficult for the visitor to find the information they seek. You are much better off having a one or two page website with no more information on it than your brochure, than you are having a multi-paged website that is too complicated to navigate. Keeping it simple in the early days is best for everyone.

I'm not a website builder or designer, so this chapter is not about the technical side of website creation; it's a basic checklist so you can get underway.

First and foremost you will need to decide on, and then buy, a domain name. The domain is the name of the website, such as belindagrace.com. There is a lot of debate about whether or not your domain name should say something about your product or service, for example clairvoyanthealing.com, but choosing a domain name is not a one-size-fits-all conversation. You will need to decide for yourself what you like and what you believe works. The major work of promoting your website will be done via all your other marketing activities and search engine optimisation (SEO), which should be built into your website from day one. Good SEO means that when people are browsing the internet using key words that apply to your service, they are more likely to find your website.

Once you have chosen a domain name you can register that separately through a domain name registry such as www.godaddy.com or www.netregistry. com. These types of companies are now so numerous that you really need to shop around. Ask someone you trust, who already operates a website you like, who they are registered with and who hosts their website.

As mentioned above, your website will also need hosting. Put simply, the host is where your website lives. Even though your website is not a physical entity like an office or store, it still needs to reside somewhere, and this is done by hosting companies. These days you can sign up for the whole package, domain name registry, website hosting, templates and tools with which to build your own website, through one company. Please note that I am not willing to give personal recommendations for any of them and the following list is simply of well-known services that offer these packages. At time of writing, many of my peers are very happy with Squarespace, but I still recommend you shop around and compare —

www.wix.com
www.weebly.com
www.wordpress.org
www.nohasslewebsite.com
www.squarespace.com

If designing your own business cards and brochures is like going down a rabbit hole, then creating your own website and maintaining it can be like trying to navigate the entire rabbit warren. So keep a cool head, don't sign up for packages that lock you into big monthly fees for years on end and talk, talk, talk to people who are a few steps ahead of you in the process. The world of website creation is always changing and it's not possible to keep up unless that's your profession or passion. Just be clear on what your website needs to do for you and stay focused on that. Then please hire someone to help you with creating good SEO for your website. So that people will find you when they are browsing.

When someone visits your website they will want to see a picture of you, some pictures that tell them what you do and the minimum number of words that clearly convey your message. They will want to know when and where you are available, how much your services cost and a little bit about you, in the form of a short biography. Always remember that your website is about what you can do for your clients.

I would definitely recommend buying a website package that is e-commerce or woo-commerce ready. This means that you can create a shop on your site when you have virtual products, like a workshop, or physical products, like candles, to sell later as your business develops.

Last but not least, it is very worthwhile setting up Google Analytics on your site, from day one. Analytics are all about how many people are visiting your site, what pages they are looking at and how much time they spend there. It can also provide you with fascinating information such as what devices people are using to view your site, e.g. a PC or smartphone and what channel brought them to your website, e.g. an organic search on Google or links from your Facebook page or Instagram. All of this information may seem like overkill in the beginning when you only have a handful of clients and a two-page website, but if you install it from the get-go you won't have to do it later and you'll have the full history so you can compare the effects of any changes you make.

Always keep your website current with up-to-date contact details, pricing and availability. Also include something useful on your site like a beautiful quote, the dates of upcoming events or even the next full moon. Keep your website interesting so that visitors will want to stay and return.

While a visitor is on your website they should be prompted to join your mailing list. A mailing list is incredibly important and the most effective way to stay in touch with the people who are interested in what you do. Please set up your mailing list/ newsletter sign-up, from day one. If you are not collecting people's email addresses and staying in touch with them regularly then you are doing yourself a huge disservice.

Facebook and Instagram are both platforms that are easy to use and can be very worthwhile. They are both free to use unless you choose to boost or create ads. So why not put your practice out there? It's important to understand that your business page needs to be exactly that. It's one of those Facebook pages that visitors can 'Like' and 'Follow', not one where they send you a 'Friend' request. In the early days of my practice I didn't understand the difference and only created a personal page where people could 'Friend' me. So now I have my personal page and my business page and have to manage and use them both to promote my services. I don't mind doing this, but it would have been a lot cleaner and simpler if I had kept my personal page for family and friends (people I actually know) and my business page for everyone else. Make sure you comb through all the options on Facebook before setting up your page.

There are many companies and online groups offering Facebook and Instagram tutorials these days. They can show you how to make your pages stand out and maximise your potential for attracting new clients. They all make it sound like a simple formula that will have new clients beating your door down, but it usually takes a lot more time and effort than that. If you are a Mac user then your local Mac store may offer some classes or put you onto local companies that do. Also check out your local community colleges because they can be an amazing source of affordable education.

Generally speaking the idea with Facebook is to attract as many 'Likes' and 'Follows' to your page as possible in order to increase your audience. You then engage with them by putting up regular posts about anything that may interest or excite them, e.g. a two-for-one bonus or a special offer for Christmas. The vast majority of your posts should be accompanied by at least one great image that relates to the topic and is eye-catching.

Instagram is another interesting platform, especially as more and more people are doing all their browsing, research, messaging and reading on their smartphones. I like the simplicity of Instagram. It's visual, quick, you only need a short caption and you can include plenty of hashtags # to attract new viewers to your feed. So for example I use hashtags like #angels, #clairvoyant, #intuition, #pastlives, #chakras, #spirituality and #highestpath. This means that when someone is browsing Instagram through those key words, they are likely to find your post and will hopefully start following you. I am not sure if Instagram was originally designed with sales in mind, but it's increasingly working that way for me, with visitors placing book orders and booking in for workshops after seeing my Instagram posts. You can set up your own Instagram account by downloading their app directly to your smartphone.

Now that you are bristling with marketing material your business will start to grow. One of the big skills with websites and social media is weeding out the time wasters. You will soon learn to detect the people who want to sell you something, tell you all their troubles and life story without ever booking in to see you, or who are looking for free advice. If anyone is ever rude to you or uses your page to promote their own agendas, businesses or products, you can block them. For both

Facebook and Instagram please make that extra effort to put security settings in place at time of set-up. The options are quite clearly explained on their respective websites, so it's more just a matter of taking the time to understand how, and if you aren't sure you can contact their help desks and ask.

#Goodluck!

Creating an online presence and practising online

Depending on your modality it may be possible for you to develop an online client base in addition to your in-person practice. This can be very exciting and can really help to expand your practice. I began doing readings by telephone, back in 2005, and they became much more popular after my first book *You Are Clairvoyant* was published in 2007, as readers from all over Australia began to contact me. Initially, I was very nervous about doing readings in this way because I believed that the manner of communication would reduce the quality of the connection between the client and me and therefore reduce the quality of the guidance I could provide. Really I had no choice though. If I wanted to respond to my readers who could not come to Sydney to see me, I had to use the phone.

Looking back now I laugh about the technology I used at the time. I used a landline phone on loudspeaker and recorded the reading on a cassette tape that I would post to the client. It all worked perfectly well and to my astonishment my clients were very happy with their readings, came back for more and recommended their friends. Almost overnight I went from being a Sydney-based practitioner with a Sydney-based clientele to a practitioner with a national, and soon to be international, clientele. I loved it!

The year 2007 now seems like a long time ago and most people these days are more than happy to communicate via Skype, FaceTime, WhatsApp and so on. It's incredible to me that so many of these forms of unlimited communication are free, as long as you have internet access. Occasionally, I still have a client who doesn't want to use or try Skype or similar, so I call them on the phone wherever they are in the world for next to no cost. Amazing!

My international client base arose mainly out of three things, my website and social media presence, my books being published across more and more countries and my willingness to travel. I should also acknowledge word of mouth here, okay so that's four things, because as soon as my clients discovered that I could do readings via telephone and Skype they began sending their overseas friends and family members to me, as well. It was exponential.

There are so many ways to build a national and international client base these days because the internet has very few borders. So it's up to you and how adventurous you'd like to be. For many of my graduates, working online was a natural and obvious step because they had migrated to Australia earlier in life and still had many people back in their home country that wanted to experience their work. So sometimes your lifestyle and circumstances will make working online a relatively easy option for you.

Your website will be key in attracting clients for long-distance consultations and readings, so it's worth going back to the topic of SEO quality. You can have a great looking website with loads of excellent offerings, but if no one finds it then it's not paying its way. If the idea of doing consultations or readings online bothers you then go back to that beginner's philosophy of offering free sessions for a set period of time. Then offer low-cost sessions for a set period of time to help you attract clients and build your skills and confidence. You are translating your skills from one medium to another so this will affect the way you deliver the information and the way the client receives it. This leap of translation is one of the reasons I prefer a visual medium, like Skype or FaceTime, to the telephone, because I can see my client, they can see me, and I can demonstrate things visually when necessary.

If your modality doesn't translate well to online consultations you can still grow your internet presence with a blog and by selling products you have created, such as an eBook, or products you endorse and distribute such as bamboo pillows or essential oils. We'll talk more in a later chapter about expanding your product range and creating more income streams, though.

Another great way to develop an online client base is to offer online follow-up consultations and mentoring programs. Say, for example, you are a naturopath or nutritionist. Your client comes in for a consultation or two and you begin to get their health and diet on track. Do they need to keep coming back and paying a full fee for an in-person consultation? Maybe not, and maybe you can free up your face-to-face time for clients who need it and will pay that higher premium to see you in person. You have established a connection and working relationship with your return clients and can now suggest, if it's appropriate to their healing pathway, that you can check in with each other online regularly until they are back in full health, with the option of returning in person if things take a different turn. Your clients will at the very least appreciate the options, and many of them will jump at the opportunity because you will be saving them travel time and money.

This concept works particularly well if you are willing and able to travel with your work. There is no need to lose contact with the clients you see in each location if they can take up an ongoing program with you once you're gone. The program does not need to be long and costly, maybe just one or two follow-up calls within a set time period. Be creative and offer a few different packages to discover what your clients want.

If you are only ever going to meet your client online then it's important to ask them for some basic information before commencing the consultation. I have many clients who I've never met in person; this works just fine for clairvoyant readings because I receive the same guidance, answers and images for them whether we are in the same room or on opposite sides of the world. On my website I have a page dedicated to Skype and telephone readings which includes a form for the client to fill out when they would like to book. Naturally, I ask for their name and contact details but I also always request a photo because that helps me to make a connection to them before we get online. It's also professional because if for some reason the vision doesn't work on the day, or we have to resort to telephone contact, I like to know what they look like and have a sense of the person I am talking with. So please don't rely on saying 'I'll be able to see what they look like once we get online' because none of these platforms are infallible, and if there is a thunderstorm going on outside you don't want to lose your client.

I would like to mention a word about payment. When doing readings online or by phone, even with return clients, I ask for payment in advance. Why? Because whether we like to admit it or not, in our culture money equals commitment. Time and again I have found that if the client hasn't paid for their appointment in advance they are more likely to forget, be late or cancel. That was years ago, and I don't do that anymore because my time is important and so is yours. When a client has paid in advance they will remember, be punctual and only reschedule if they absolutely have to. That makes a big difference to your self-esteem, income and professional time.

How do my clients pay me if we never meet in person? Good question! I simply send them an invoice via PayPal, which gives them the option of paying from their own PayPal account or paying by credit card. If they have an Australian bank account they can also pay me by electronic funds transfer or EFT, and if they are outside Australia they can still pay into my bank account via TransferWise. So there are plenty of options.

Another tool I find invaluable is a website called www.timeanddate.com I love this site and would struggle to keep my schedule without it. This free and very clever website allows you to use a meeting planner function whereby you add in the cities that you and your clients are in, plus the date. Then their system shows you the times and dates in each location so you can be sure that you won't have to get up at 3 am to keep an appointment. Believe me, I've done it! It takes the guesswork out of international consultations.

When I am travelling, which is often five months of the year, I use this website daily to check everything on my schedule, from flights to catching up with family and friends back home.

I would like to encourage you to think outside the square so you can consult with a wider client base online. Then you can have a wonderful selection of options for your clients and that other important spice of life for yourself, variety. Use your website and social media platforms to promote your online availability, be sure to mention it in your brochures and tell your local clients. These days everyone seems to have a friend or family member living in another country and in this email, internet age news travels fast.

CHAPTER TEN

JOINING AN EXISTING PRACTICE

There are some golden rules to be aware of when approaching a professional centre as a new practitioner. So if you want to expand your business and raise your profile you will have much greater success with this inside information.

Over the last twenty years I have worked in several different complementary health centres, and I have seen would-be and new practitioners make the same mistakes over and over again. So let's cover each of them and have you feeling confident.

If you haven't started looking already then it might be time to begin shopping around in your area and combing the internet for places of interest. If there are several in your area, or within comfortable commuting distance, then you might want to make a shortlist of your favourites. They should be in a location that is conducive to the kind of services they are offering and your modality is already on offer there or will be one that complements what they already have on offer. For example, they may have three different styles of massage and a naturopath but no osteopathy, acupuncture, Reiki or chakra balancing. So be on the lookout for these types of opportunities.

My preferred approach is to drop in and ask to see the practice manager or owner, or to phone and make an appointment with him or her. Dropping in unannounced can be very interesting because you will get an overview of the atmosphere and levels of service without them initially knowing why you are there. This can be a good snapshot and give you an honest sense of what it might be like to work from there. If you feel a bit nervous about just showing up, remember that any good practice is always interested in talking to someone with talent and initiative. You clearly have talent, right? Otherwise you wouldn't have that lovely diploma or degree hanging on your wall, and you have initiative, enough to get yourself into their reception area to make an enquiry.

If you do drop in without an appointment please make sure you take along a copy of your qualification and a very brief CV, complete with your phone number and email address. Your CV must include some information about what you have been doing to grow your client base since you graduated, so that they can see you have already made a start. Leave your CV with them even if they don't seem too interested at the time. There are many reasons why they may not instantly roll out the red carpet for you, the main one being that they are probably very busy people. So be polite, persistent and don't take any initial brusqueness personally. You haven't proved yourself yet.

More often than not, you will get a warm welcome and someone will come and speak with you for a few minutes. This is where you can hand over your CV and gauge whether or not a fuller appointment would be beneficial. Find out if they have any rooms free and on what days, and if the conversation can continue you may be able to ask about rental fees. They may even give you a rental contract to take home and look over. Most centres will expect you to give the owner or manager a free session before taking you on, so that at least one person in the business knows exactly how you work and can personally recommend you.

Another common response is that there are no rooms available at this time. That may well be true in that moment, but if you really like that particular place just be positive and leave your CV with them anyway. Even in successful, busy, natural health centres there can be a regular turnover of practitioners. Peoples' lives and circumstances are always changing and what the receptionist tells you on Monday may have completely changed by Tuesday. A good practice manager or owner knows this and is always on the lookout for practitioners, even when their rooms are currently full.

After you have had a brief chat and left your CV it is extremely important to follow up with emails and/or by phone. Don't just wait and expect them to call you. The centre I still work from in Sydney whenever I'm in town, averages one to two people a day coming in and asking about a room. They don't have time to call them all. It's up to you. If you like the feel of the centre and can see yourself doing well there then you have to keep reminding them that you are keen.

The biggest mistake new practitioners make when starting at an established centre is to imagine that the centre will expand your client base for you. Don't fall into this trap! It doesn't matter how busy, supportive and well meaning they are, in the early days the referrals will not be enough. Building a relationship with the owner and other practitioners will take time, months in fact, so banking on in-house referrals to sustain you is not the way to go. It will make you seem unprofessional and burdensome.

You need to understand that you, and you alone, are responsible for attracting clients and developing your own client base. If you haven't started doing this yet then please refer back to Chapter Eight and get that ball rolling. It always takes much longer than anticipated to build a solid client base, complete with return clients and referrals. So the time to start is now. When a prospective centre owner or manager can see that you are making the effort in this department you will stand head and shoulders above most other applicants.

One of the keys to succeeding in a busy practice is the ability to put yourself in their shoes. They are not sitting around waiting for you to drop in and offer your services, they are not there to coach you or comfort you when your business is slow. A well-run centre will be supportive but they are already working long hours balancing the needs of all their practitioners, dealing with clients and administering the business itself. It's a seven-day-a-week job. They will be looking for someone who is an asset to their business and who can bring new clientele in, because the other practitioners would one day love to receive referrals from you.

If all goes well and you are invited to join them, there are a few things you want to be very clear on before you sign on the dotted line.

How much is your total rent daily? Weekly? Monthly? Including all relevant taxes.

What does your rent include? Reception services? Computerised appointment system? Confirmation calls or SMS to clients?

Does the rent always increase at a certain time of year, such as the end of financial year, or is each contract individually negotiable? What can you do if you don't agree with the amount of the increase?

Will your details be included on their website and Facebook page? Will your arrival at the centre be mentioned in their next newsletter?

What equipment and furniture are provided, and what do you need to supply?

Will you have a designated, secure storage space at the centre?

What is the exact time your shift begins and ends? When do you need to be out of the room?

Will you have a key? Will you be charged a fee for the key and a fee to replace it if you lose it?

Can you access the centre and your room, outside normal business hours, for early or late appointments?

Is there a small tea-making or kitchen facility? What are the rules regarding storage in, and usage of, this area?

Is the centre open seven days? Are there any days or evenings with large groups, noisy events etc. that might disrupt your work?

Are the rooms air-conditioned and heated, and who controls that? Are there separate fans and portable heaters available to adjust the room temperature to your own liking, or can you supply those?

What is their policy regarding music in the common areas, reception and in the rooms? Who controls that?

What are their busiest times of the week, month and year? What are their slowest times of the week, month, and year?

As you can see from the list above, there can be a lot to consider, but don't let it overwhelm you. You may not want to enquire about all of the above before signing, but I would recommend at least observing what you can and asking about what is not obvious to the naked eye. It really is best not to take anything for granted. In my experience, it's everyday things such as the preset temperature of the air-conditioning or the disruption of people chatting in the reception area that can be the seemingly trivial things that drive people crazy.

The contract — Many centres will ask you to sign a rental contract, usually for a minimum of six months with a requirement of thirty days' notice if you decide to leave. This means that you will have to pay rent for a minimum of six months even if you decide to leave before that time is up. This is fair enough. The centre and its staff will be investing time in you and may have turned down other practitioners to let you have that room. They are running a business with ongoing costs, and you need to understand that.

Once the contract has expired some centres will put you on a month-by-month basis, where both parties are required to give the other thirty days notice to quit, and other centres will ask you to sign another contract. The contract can also work in your favour, meaning that they must give you notice, so you have time to make other arrangements if they need you to leave. The contract can also lock you into a set rent and help you avoid rental price rises for the period of the contract.

My suggestion is to never sign up for more than six months. That is enough time for both parties to ascertain whether or not the working relationship is a good one, and it is enough time for you to start establishing yourself.

It is a very good idea to consider the worst-case scenario before signing, meaning that if your six months at the centre was not good for your business, could you still pay the rent for six months? Will your other job cover this expense, or do you have the money in the bank? Are you prepared to pay this if necessary? Am I being all doom and gloom here? No, not at all. This is one of my key strategies whenever I consider doing something that could be risky. I ask myself 'What is the worst-case scenario if I proceed, and can I live with it?' So be honest with yourself before making the commitment, and you will feel much more centred and confident.

There is another approach, which is popular with some centres and practitioners. This is the 'pay a percentage of what you earn' approach, meaning that if you have no clients that day you don't pay any rent or you only pay an agreed minimum. I am a big fan of this system when I'm travelling and giving workshops and readings in each location for only a few days, because it motivates the venue to fill up my schedule with readings and my workshops with students. The busier I am the more they earn and it also means I don't have to commit large sums of money up front. I know that they'll book me up and they know they'll get paid. So it's a win-win situation when I'm on the move.

However I am not such a fan of this system when it relates to somewhere I want to establish my practice and be in the longer term. Human psychology is a peculiar thing and I have seen this within myself, other practitioners and graduates. If your monkey mind knows that you are off the hook, it will have an impact on your motivation. It's as simple as that. Whether you know it or not, most of us thrive on healthy challenges and need some positive pressure to get us moving. Yes, there is such a thing as positive pressure! So, if you know you have to pay that rent, come what may, something in you will rise to the challenge and you will succeed more rapidly. It's human nature.

Yes, the centre will be more motivated to generate bookings for you if they can only bill you for a percentage of what you earn, but the reality is that they cannot pluck clients out of thin air, and they should be busy looking after all the other practitioners too, not to mention the needs of the constant stream of clients. So don't ignore the obvious pitfall here. All their attention and energy will not be focused on you, irrespective of their good intentions.

A good way to budget for your first three months is to expect to have no clients at all for two out of the four or five weeks in the month, and then for your next three months budget for an absence of clients for one week per month. If you are not seeing at least one paying client a week by your sixth month, then you need to review your strategies and ask yourself what needs to change, or what needs to be done better. Ideally you will be even busier than that, but there will be more about this in the coming chapter 'Dont Be Afraid to Make Mistakes'.

So you feel ready to sign a contract. You have read Chapter Five about how much to charge and how that should relate to your room costs, and you have discussed the main points from the list above with the practice owner or manager. Great! But there are a few more very important things to consider.

Your commencement date is an important consideration. Avoid starting your business on or just before big public holidays, school holidays and summer breaks. Whilst this is a generalisation, it is usually true that even the busier practitioners are quiet at this time.

If this is your only option or the only one you are being offered, you might be able to negotiate cheaper rent or percentage only for that period, for example over Christmas and New Year in Australia, Summer Break and the 4th of July holiday in the USA and the July/August holiday season in the UK and Europe.

What days of the week are you signing up for? For example, Tuesday morning will probably be a lot quieter than Saturday morning. Thursday, Friday and Saturday are usually the busiest days in most centres.

Clarify once more what system is in place for taking appointments. Who will take the bookings and how will you notify each other? This will save you the embarrassment of two clients arriving for the same timeslot, or you not being there when a client arrives. It happens!

When you are happy with all of the above, you'll be as informed as possible and making an intelligent choice rather than a hope-for-the-best-guess. Business is not about guesswork and you didn't invest all those years and dollars studying in order to be disappointed. You have something excellent to offer and it's time for you to bring it to the world.

I would like to mention a note on attendance. I am a big fan of being present at the centre irrespective of whether I have bookings in advance or not. These days I am fully booked wherever I go, Gracias a la Diosa!, but it was a very different story all those years ago. I had made that commitment, so in I went because I know that energy and intention are very powerful. So be punctual, be present for all your shifts and be ready for success. Your next client could walk in the door any minute, and they may just turn out to be the one who returns regularly and sends all their friends.

If your start date is ASAP, that can be fun and very exciting, but there can be advantages to having a little lead time. The centre you are going to work at must have some type of internet presence and a regular way of reaching out to clients, such as an email newsletter. At the very least, part of your deal with them, and part of what you are paying your rent for, is the online promotion. So please be sure that you have enough time to provide them with your information and a nice photo, and they have enough time to upload it to their website and Facebook page and to mention the presence of you and your modality at their wonderful centre. Once this is complete and you have checked that it's all been done – promises to put your details up on the website at some point are not good enough – you will have covered all the bases you can before getting started.

Make sure that you have your own online promotions ready to post, put your brochures in reception, pin them up on all your local community notice boards, tell all your friends and stay upbeat. You are well and truly on your way.

CHAPTER ELEVEN

DON'T BE AFRAID TO MAKE MISTAKES

My angels and spirit guides often say that there is no such thing as a mistake, only experience and experiment. They say that the closest we come in life to making mistakes is when we insist on doing the same things over and over again while expecting a different result. So if you find that something in your practice isn't working, it's much better to be open about it and learn from it. Making a mistake is not the problem at all. It's just another opportunity to learn. The problems only arise if you ignore the signs or refuse to take a look at what you might need to change.

There are numerous ways in which your fledgling practice could fail, and you are reading this book in order to help you avoid those major pitfalls. You are doing your research, and that effort will be rewarded for many years to come. Being open to learning new things and new ways of doing them, is crucial. So don't be afraid to make mistakes, they are opportunities to improve and succeed. If you follow the steps and suggestions in this book, you will have a much greater chance of making your practice a success, but there is no book on the planet that can provide all the answers for your own unique circumstance.

One of the most interesting aspects of human nature is the way in which many people live simply to limit their exposure to disappointment. You are not one of those people because you have been courageous enough to come this far and want to explore the road less travelled. Anyone can warn you about what might go wrong, and caution you against living outside the square, but you learn more about yourself and grow more as a person when you take that step beyond. Mistakes and disappointments, therefore, may be almost inevitable, so here is the positive twist. If you try something that doesn't work you can cross it off your list and try something else. This is the approach I have taken in my practice for over twenty years.

Being flexible and remaining positive is so important because the unexpected always happens in small business and in life. If I had insisted on staying in a certain groove with my courses for example, I may never have made the leap to running the five-day residential intensives. I was very happy with, and attached to, the pattern of running my courses as weekly classes in Sydney, and for many years this worked well for everyone. But I became increasingly aware of the people who lived outside of Sydney and also the people within Sydney who were struggling to attend evening classes after a long day at work. On the face of it, my weekly classes were starting to fail, but I chose to see it as the chance to succeed in a different way. The result being that I have been running the five-day residential courses for eight years, they are always fully booked and I love doing them.

If you are struggling at that basic financial level of not having enough clients to cover your costs then your first step could be to go back through this book and notice what you have overlooked. You'll need to be very honest with yourself because pretending or ignoring isn't going to solve the problem. If you haven't printed your brochures yet, or you are only offering consultations at home, then maybe people just aren't hearing about you or aren't able to get to you. Maybe you aren't charging enough; maybe you are paying too much rent at the professional centre or maybe the centre already has several other practitioners offering what you do. Some centres are guilty of this, so avoid this trap at all costs. Go back and do your homework until you discover what you have missed or notice what you need to change.

Managing your own expectations is important too. One of the main things that new practitioners underestimate is the length of time it will take for their business to become viable. For me it took about three years of working in the same professional centre before I could really sense a loyal client base, but it took ten years before I was able to give up all other forms of work and rely solely on the income I receive from readings, courses, workshops and product royalties. So please be realistic, otherwise you will be doing yourself and your practice a disservice.

When we fail at something we are often brought face to face with our own lack of confidence. Even if you are confident in other areas of life this can be different because the business of being a practitioner is very personal. In one sense you become the product, the business and the brand. If lack of confidence is part of your challenge then please reach out for support. You can receive support from books, online information and forums, Facebook groups, the peers and friends you committed to staying in touch with back at the beginning of this book, family members, mentors and coaches. Availing yourself of any of these options is not just an investment in your business, it's an investment in yourself.

Whenever the world doesn't deliver what we want and/or believe we deserve or have earned, it is the universe's way of saying 'There is something you need to be more aware of here.' In my work as a clairvoyant healer I so often find that there is a past-life issue with abundance, oaths of poverty, aversion to success/drawing attention to yourself, fear of failure or a traumatic experience of being punished or ostracised when trying to offer healing modalities in less enlightened times hundreds of years ago. The changes that have occurred in my students' and clients' lives after releasing these old patterns, have been staggering. I have witnessed everything from being able to conceive after years of fruitless attempts with IVF to breakthroughs in confidence and success in their practices.

If you feel drawn to the path of investigating your past lives and the impact they are having on you today, you can discover more in my book *You Are Clairvoyant*, or by having a personal reading, taking my online course or attending one of my courses in person. Please see my website for details. There are many other excellent practitioners of past-life investigation and clearing those old patterns, so you don't have to work with me, but this is what I have to offer.

If you don't feel that you are succeeding, the universe isn't trying to punish you, it's just trying to get your attention. So please look upon any so-called failure with a new perspective. It's all about how you choose to see things and how you choose to respond. One of my personal mantras in life is that 'I go where the doors open.' Years ago I would expend my energy trying to shove through the doors that remained stubbornly closed, trying to enforce my will on my life.

Those early years of my practice when I wanted only to be a homoeopath are a case in point. Understandable enough to a degree – I had just spent four years studying homoeopathy – but it was the chakra balancing that people wanted from me, that's what they came back for. So I learned that my 'failure' as a homeopath was simply the door opening to being a clairvoyant healer.

Success is always a combination of doing what is required, being consistent, perseverance and listening to your intuition. You create a structure that you, your clients and your colleagues can understand, and then within that structure you add your own personal creativity and magic. That's how you create your niche, and if you persevere whilst doing what feels right in your heart, then you will succeed.

CHAPTER TWELVE

GREAT SERVICE WILL KEEP THEM COMING BACK

The very core of my practice is built on good customer service. It is something I am passionate about. It's so simple and can be the difference between your success or failure as a practitioner. This should only need to be a short chapter because it should be obvious, but unfortunately we find less and less good, personal service in most businesses these days. Good service is one of the ways we can make our industry shine because no amount of fancy gadgets, do-it-yourself kits or online programs can replace a great personal experience. Yes, over time you will carve out your own unique niche, but even if you are the only person on the planet offering your unique gifts, good customer service brings many rewards.

Chief among them of course is your own sense of pride and the satisfaction you will derive from knowing you have done all you can to assist your clients within the high standards of your professional boundaries. Good customer service doesn't mean that you have to answer your phone on Sundays or reply to emails until midnight. You have a life too, and sane people will respect that.

Good customer service is a simple formula – treat people how you would like to be treated. No one likes waiting days for a reply when they are eager for more information or simply want to make a booking. Depending on your modality, your prospective clients may even be ill or in pain, so it's vital that you have a system that is workable for you and delivers great response times to your clientele. My general rule of thumb is to reply to all emails within 48 hours, stretching a tiny bit for emails received late on Friday, which might not be answered until Monday morning. If a client phones me and leaves a message, I usually call them back same day but certainly within 24 hours.

Please make sure that you have an appropriate message on your mobile phone so that callers know that it's you they have reached and whether or not they should leave you a message. Email autoresponders can be a good idea, especially if you are going away and can't, or don't want to, answer emails during that time. If you are working from a professional centre, always make sure that the receptionist is aware of any changes to your availability, and make sure that you are clear about how client messages will be handled. Will the centre contact you with the clients' details or do you need to phone in or email reception daily/regularly to retrieve your messages?

All of these added touches of professionalism, good communication and organisation will be felt by the client, to some degree, and could save you a lot of confusion or embarrassment. Please be sure to treat your receptionists, answering services and booking staff with the respect they deserve. They are not answering machines or mind readers! Incredible as it may seem I have, over the years, observed so many practitioners who imagine that the receptionist is there to trail around after them, remember things for them and fix their fumbles. A helpful receptionist may do that once or twice, but they will soon become impatient with you if you don't take a moment to understand the kind of pressure they are under. I've always admired good receptionists because it's a job I simply could not do. In my view, a person who can be polite whilst answering phones, emails and the same kind of questions day in day out, whilst keeping track of everyone's needs along the way, is worth their weight in gold.

If you are going to take all your own bookings you may want to consider offering an appointment scheduling system on your website. In this era of booking our own flights and hotels online, most people can cope with booking an appointment through such a system, but there will always be someone who can't or won't use it. So, if you would like to encourage them, you will still need to be accessible by email or phone. Your job is to make sure your system works fluidly and that your schedule is kept up to date.

A word about consistency — for me this is a vital part of the good customer service picture that is often trivialised or overlooked. Your clients will appreciate, and your business will benefit from, consistency. I'll say it again — consistency. So what is consistency and why is it so important? It is reliable, knowable behaviour, a pattern or schedule that people can grasp and even memorise. It's important because the vast majority of people are creatures of habit and live within a schedule of their own. So if you keep changing the days or hours that you are available, it will confuse people, cause them to lose track of you and possibly even lose confidence in you, because you might seem — dare I say it — inconsistent. And that is not a quality clients are looking for in a practitioner.

By using the information in this book and your own plentiful common sense, you will make the best choices you can about how to launch and maintain your practice. Changes are inevitable at some point. It's not about locking yourself in and throwing away the key. It's about awareness. You don't want to come across as flaky. So when you commit to certain days of the week or month at a holistic health centre, local market or festival, be sure to look through your calendar for the next six to twelve months to make sure that those commitments don't clash with holidays, anniversaries or other events that may tempt you to rearrange your availability.

If you are consistent and reliable your clients will have more faith in you, feel more secure and even rearrange their plans to fit in with your schedule. You can't ask for more than that. All of the above also applies when working from home, especially if it's your only location at present. If home is a backup to your hours at a centre, please make it clear that seeing you at home encompasses more fluid hours and is done individually by mutual arrangement.

Punctuality is another big issue for new practitioners, and not just yours, the clients' too. When you are just starting out you will probably accommodate your clients' timing like they are royalty, but it really is best to begin as you mean to go on. Project yourself forward to five years from now, when you are in demand and have clients booked in back-to-back appointments all day. If you only have the one appointment in your six-hour shift, then a client being twenty minutes late doesn't seem so bad, but when you have several clients with only a few minutes between each appointment, it can cause havoc.

First and foremost I do everything in my power to be punctual. I usually arrive at least half an hour before my shift starts so I can make the room look nice and not be scurrying around when the client arrives. One of the most difficult things for me was learning to finish the session on time after the client was late, meaning that they are receiving a shorter session than they pay for. Whether we like it or not there will always be traffic jams, public transport dramas, difficulty parking or the dog getting out just as your client tries to leave home. By all means be sympathetic to their situation, but if their tardiness means that you will be late for your next client, or that you will have to rush to, or cancel, your own important engagements, then you need to firmly and politely let the client know that a) you can't go over time for them and b) they still have to pay the full fee. It's not your fault they were late!

If you find yourself running late – we are all human and it does happen – this is when it's great to have the contact details of at least your first client of the day. Call, SMS or email them to let them know you are on your way and don't rely on the receptionist arriving early or figuring out your predicament. If you are seeing clients at home it's even more important to garner your client's email address and cell phone number when you take the booking so you can make last minute contact if need be.

All of the above is practise and habit. By starting out with good habits and practices you will not only feel more relaxed and confident, your clients will really appreciate your respect for their time, and learn to respect yours. Time is precious in so many ways and it makes sense to honour it.

Great customer service doesn't only revolve around consistency and punctuality. Thank goodness I hear you cry! There are so many simple and inexpensive ways to impress your clients and keep them coming back — like having a glass of water ready for them on arrival and asking them if they need to use the restroom before you commence. So use your imagination, be creative and make your client's time with you positive and enjoyable.

CHAPTER THIRTEEN

PROFESSIONAL BOUNDARIES FOR A PROFESSIONAL PRACTICE

There are so many ways in which you need to take care of yourself when working as a practitioner. If your professional role is to guide people to better health and happiness then it stands to reason that *you* also need to be healthy and happy. If you are run ragged and stressed about time and finances, it's going to show up in your work and have a major impact on your personal life. Running your own small business comes with challenges and that's simply a fact, but there are plenty of ways you can minimise the potential stresses and keep the challenges interesting and positive.

I cannot emphasise strongly enough how important it is to establish these boundaries from the beginning. Setting healthy precedents and starting the way you mean to continue, will make all of your life much more enjoyable. Looking back on my twenty years of practice, I wish someone had sat me down and told me these things because the first ten years were very stressful, and I learned most of the wisdom I'm about to outline here, by making the mistakes first. You don't need to experience that pain, so lets create some clarity around financial boundaries.

Setting financial boundaries that suit you can be extremely rewarding and leave you with a sense of peace. So they are well worth putting in place. Having a clear cancellation policy for appointments is a great way of sending a professional message to your clients. If you are taking your own bookings by phone and/or email you can SMS your client a confirmation of the time and date, along with your cancellation policy, or email it to them. I encourage you to request payments in full or a 50 per cent deposit at the time of booking. This creates a little more administration work for you but it will give you peace of mind. Your time is valuable and you are too busy to wait all afternoon for someone who doesn't show up.

You may wish to consider an even more high-tech option and have all bookings go via your website where full payment or a deposit are required to complete the booking. Even if that feels a little way down the road for you, it's still worth considering — it's good to think ahead and think big. Make your cancellation policy very clear in your SMS, email and on your website.

A generally accepted standard is that if the client cancels with less than 24 hours notice they will forfeit their deposit, and of course, if they are a no-show they will also forfeit whatever prepayment they have made, irrespective of their reasons.

This may sound a little harsh, but when you have driven all the way to the centre to see them, or tidied up your home to welcome them and they don't turn up, it can be extremely demoralising and costly. Rescheduling is a bit of a grey area and needs to be addressed on a case-by-case basis. I recommend that if you are going to accept their request to reschedule and allow them to transfer their prepayment to the new appointment, then the client must book in for a specific date and time. A vague promise to come and see you some time in the future is not good enough. They either forfeit their payment or they make a firm booking for another day. The ideal scenario is that you keep 50 per cent for the time that you have lost, and they reschedule and still pay the full amount for the subsequent appointment.

Sometimes these policies are difficult to enforce and may put people off. If you have never seen a client before and you didn't secure a deposit for their booking, there is probably nothing you can do, after they cancel or no-show, to recoup your loss. At the very least, by creating and communicating a clear cancellation policy you will be sending a message that you aren't just an amateur and this isn't just a hobby. This can be one of the major pitfalls of working from home. Clients may choose to perceive that this is only a hobby for you or that punctuality isn't as crucial because "You are at home today anyway aren't you?" It can take a while before you find balance in all of these matters.

You can also use the opportunity to create goodwill between you and your clients by agreeing to waive the forfeit 'just this once' as long as they make another firm booking. By letting them off once, you engender goodwill and give yourself another opportunity to highlight the fact that it has cost you time and money to prepare for them and that this is your business. Employed people who have never run their own business rarely give any thought to the fact that an appointment lost can never be replaced. You can never have that day and time again, and just rescheduling doesn't really solve the problem. It's great that the client still genuinely wants to see you but what about the hour that wasn't filled and the rent you still have to pay at that professional centre? Imagine if an employed person went to work and their boss told them "Oh we don't have much work for you to do today so we are only going to pay you for seven hours instead of eight. Sorry we didn't think to let you know earlier." They would not be impressed! Time lost is time lost and it can never be replaced. Rescheduling is better than completely losing the client but it still means that you will have to find time for them somewhere else.

I once had to turn away a client who arrived over an hour late, because I had another client scheduled on Skype. He was late because he had forgotten about the time difference between the state I live in, here in Australia, and the state he drove in from. He had my number but didn't call me because he thought that as I 'was only working from home' it wouldn't matter. So when I told him I was fully booked that day, he was shocked. I felt for him and the fact that he had driven for over two hours to come to see me but it was out of my hands.

Cancellation policies are worthwhile when working from a professional centre as well. So check with the centre. Do they have a general policy that covers all their practitioners, or are you required to create and request one of your own? Some centres won't like the idea of taking deposits in advance because their reception is already so busy. So that approach can be inconvenient in this setting. Discuss the issue of cancellations and policies with the owner, manager and other practitioners. My experience has been that I have fewer cancellations when working from a centre than I do when working from home because I have specific and limited availability at the centre. Clients know they may have to wait some time before another opportunity and they perceive it as a much more businesslike commitment. I almost always have a waiting list as well, so that if someone does cancel at the last minute, the receptionist quickly fills that place from the waiting list.

I recommend that you clearly underline the professional nature of your work whenever you can. So at the very least, at the time of booking, the receptionist could mention that you have a 50 per cent cancellation fee for cancellations under 24 hours. If you have never worked with that client before, and they don't reschedule, you probably won't ever see that money, but it's still good for your overall presentation to have it, and returning clients will be more aware. On the odd occasion I have even emailed or (in the old days) posted an invoice to a client after a no-show and a few of them did contact me and pay, much to my amazement. Again it's not just about the money, it's about your time, effort and taking responsibility for a commitment. You deserve to be compensated when you have held up your side of the bargain.

Gift vouchers can cause another interesting grey area because for some reason the recipients always seem to use them at the last minute. I prefer a three month expiry date on my gift vouchers. Why? Because I want to motivate the recipient to use it sooner rather than later, in case I want to raise my prices or make other changes to the services I offer, such as a change of location. At times, I have had gift voucher recipients request books or attendance at one of my workshops, in place of a personal reading. I am usually happy to make that shift, but you are within your rights to say that the gift voucher is only applicable for the intended product. I have never been asked for a refund on a gift voucher, again that would have to be considered on a case-by-case basis, but generally speaking, a gift voucher should be treated like any other payment in advance.

Gift voucher recipients are also notorious for contacting you a day or two before the voucher expires and expecting you to fit them in. You are under no obligation to do that and aren't responsible for their tardiness in taking up the offer. All you can do is offer them your first available appointment. Having a gift voucher does not entitle the recipient to extraordinary treatment, so when you sell the voucher please make all of these things clear on the voucher itself, or in an additional SMS, email, document or attachment that the recipient will see. Be clear about what services or products the voucher entitles the recipient to. What, if any, expiry date will be enforced, what lead time the recipient should allow for when making a booking, what hours you are available, and, if you are superorganised, you might diarise it yourself to send the purchaser a reminder email, a month before it is due to expire.

So what if you have a situation where the client is demanding a refund? It's difficult not to take these things personally and allow yourself to feel mean or greedy. In twenty years of practice I have only ever been asked once for a refund, and after a few seconds hesitation I gave it because I wanted nothing further to do with that client. This particular client had treated her reading like a legal trial, firing questions at me at a crazy pace, expecting yes/no answers to everything and showing no desire to hear what her guidance actually wanted to say to her. It was very stressful, to say the least. So when she went back out to the reception area in a huff and told the receptionist she wanted her money back, I wasn't surprised. I answer plenty of questions during my clients' readings but this woman had treated me like an information machine. So I returned her money cheerfully, feeling sure she wouldn't 'waste her time' with me again, thank goodness!

If you have a client requesting or demanding a refund it's important to find out why. It can be very difficult to manage client expectations. To this day I have first-time clients who just assume many things about what I can and can't do or what can be achieved in the space of one hour. The vast majority of people are very reasonable. If they are not, then my view is to give them their money back and make sure they don't book in to see you again. If you read a book or watch a movie and decide you don't really like it you can't go back and ask for a refund. Sometimes you'll need to look at your services in much the same way. If someone comes to you for a massage or reading because they liked the look of your website, or a friend told them you were great, that's lovely, but it's still a qualitative, subjective and personal decision. What seems excellent and worthwhile to one person can seem lackluster to another, and the client needs to understand their responsibility in choosing to book in with you.

Your website and other publicly available material become an important backup in these situations, because if the client hasn't done their research — and it's amazing how many don't — then they have made a choice based on their own assumptions (even ignorance) of what your modality offers and is capable of delivering. Clients have a responsibility in this exchange too, and these days, with websites, Facebook pages, Instagram accounts and email enquiries, it's easy to discover a great deal about you before committing to an appointment.

Last but not least we have the topic of discounts and certain people who ask for them. At a community level in many countries we are accustomed to the reality of discounts for retirees, pensioners, the unemployed, veterans and students. These can be a wonderful marketing tool for the businesses that use them and the clients who benefit from them. Having said that, I personally do not offer discounts to any of these groups. Occasionally, an individual client will ask me, or the receptionist, if I offer discounts. If my intuition tells me it's the right thing to do, then I might drop my price by a small amount, but this is not a habit I am into.

Over the years I have learned the hard way that money is a choice. Time and again, in the early years of my practice when I was struggling financially myself, I would agree to a discount of my fee, only to find out during our conversation that the client had just bought a new car or house or was soon heading off on a holiday. It used to really shock me how that same person could be so forlorn one minute, about having to pay me for their reading, and so unabashed the next about all the other things they were happily spending their money on. I hadn't forced them to come to me for a reading, so why were they complaining about the cost? This was all part of what I had to learn about valuing myself and my work.

I never discount my readings for promotional purposes either. Everyone out there is discounting their products. It's a dull and predictable thing to do, that devalues your offerings. If you want to give your clients an incentive to return, then create a loyalty program whereby they get a special gift on their fifth, seventh or tenth visit, or some other type of enticement. Always make it a value-add rather than a discount, meaning that you will give them something special, beautiful and useful like a crystal, some herbs or a candle. Give them something nice that will remind them of you and make them smile when they use it. People love receiving gifts, so make yourself unique and special by the add-ons you offer rather than by using boring old discounts as an enticement.

Trying to anticipate all the possibilities that may arise in the course of running your practice can make your head spin, so take a deep breath and get the basics in place. Then, as your practice grows you will learn what works and feels comfortable for you and have the opportunity to gauge your clients' responses, in situ. It is very important to value your work and your time and to let your existing and prospective clients *know* you value it.

CHAPTER FOURTEEN

SETTING GOALS TO NURTURE GROWTH

We all love the excitement of starting something new. The thrill of making changes in your life, opening up to new possibilities, learning, meeting new people and discovering what you are capable of, can be intoxicating. Your mind is full of great ideas, you enjoy discussing them with your family and friends and you can see that new life of yours out there in your vision. You deserve all their encouragement and admiration. You are stepping up to live your dreams after all, and you are an inspiration.

But what happens after the initial excitement dies down? And how do you remain positive and passionate when you are just plodding along a year or two later? Over the years so many people have confided to me that they are great at starting new projects but not so great at following through, or continuing them. Why is that? Why is it that we are so willing to put time, money and energy into a new idea only to let it slip away again? It's not that you want to fail or don't care, so what is going on?

One of the main things that new practitioners don't realise about the new lifestyle they are creating is that this is a process of letting go of old habits and creating new ones. Long-term success in anything is about harnessing the power of positive habits. What often occurs is that old habits will start to creep back in after that initial flush of excitement fades away. After all your friends and family have had a free session from you, and a few paying clients have checked you out because you are the new kid on the block, you are going to have to prove to them, and to yourself, that you are in it for the long haul. For example, books don't just write themselves, and I want to continue being a published author. So, writing had to become a habit for me. I enjoy doing it but in order for writing to become a substantial part of my professional mix it had to become a habit.

We often regard habits as referring only to trivial things, such as what type of tea you prefer in the morning or your favourite shows on television, but when you really look at it, most of your life is habit. Some habits are useful and propel your life forward and some do not. In order to maintain the momentum of what you have created thus far in your practice you need to take all of those new and developing skills and actions and make them a habit. If writing was not a habit for me then maybe I would not have even completed my first book, ten years ago. I could have written half a book and then slipped back into my old habits. But I chose to make writing a habit and that is the key. So please ask yourself—what actions, attitudes and activities do you need to integrate as habits in order to keep your practice growing?

At this point in time the actions and attitudes that need to become habits may still seem awkward or challenging, such as remembering to tell your new clients about your cancellation policy, or updating your website. If you do them often enough though, they will become second nature, just like all the little habits you have integrated that allow you to drive a car, cook a meal or navigate social media.

The sheer amount of travelling I do has taught me not to enshrine my habits and put them on a pedestal, which is how many of us treat our habits. We act as though our habits are who we are. Please trust me on this, you will find that you can make a habit out of running and promoting your practice successfully for many years to come.

Another thing most people won't tell you about small business is that you are likely to have a lull, especially after the first six to twelve months. There are several key reasons for this but the main thing is to be aware that a lull will happen and to not lose heart.

A lull is natural in terms of energy and cycles. Human beings are the only creatures on the planet who think that something needs to be happening all the time and that there should always be growth. The short-term mentality of our globalised culture means that if the corporations don't make a profit every quarter then something must be drastically wrong. The truth is that in nature everything has a daily, weekly, monthly and annual cycle. We human beings forget that we are just animals and part of nature's cycles too. We forget that we are not machines. So how do we embrace the lull in a fledgling practice?

Awareness is the first step, so now that I have let the cat out of the bag you can't pretend you didn't know a lull would occur. The second step is to embrace the lull, or to use one of my favourite phrases 'go where the doors open.' The third step is to plan for the lull in advance so that it doesn't derail you financially and/or emotionally. You don't know when it may occur or how long it may last, but you can still be prepared. So let's look at a couple of examples.

You joined an existing practice after seeing friends, family and a few paying clients at home for the first few months. It all started well, especially because you had the brilliant idea of offering all the other practitioners one free session with you within the first three months of your tenure. They all jumped at the chance and promised faithfully to refer some of their clients to you because they enjoyed it so much. A few people booked in and you felt elated, but now the clients who said they would return in a few weeks haven't called back. All the other practitioners have had their free sessions and don't feel the need to return for a paid one. You put all your promotional material out there and you feel depleted. You haven't got anything new to offer. All your new stuff is out there! Believe me, this all happens, and I have been in this situation several times myself over the last two decades.

So where are the doors opening in your life? Happiness and the energy of life, refered to in general as 'The Universe', are all about balance through healthy cycles. It's at times like this, after all your beginner's luck seems to be wearing off, that you need to take a look at where you might be out of balance and take some steps to correct that. If your home life is in disarray or you haven't seen much of your friends because you have been so busy being 'Super Practitioner', then for you the lull might well be about taking some time out and attending to the other people and activities in your life that require your time. Take stock of how you feel too. Are you tired? Do you feel worn out or unwell? It's easy to ignore these things when you are bringing a new practice to life and exchanging old habits for new ones. So your solution may be to embrace the lull and use that time wisely and enjoyably for rest and relaxation.

Is there a door opening towards other things you know you need to investigate to keep expanding your business? Not all lulls are about being tired and needing a break. You may not be on the excited energy 'high' you were on when you first started at the professional centre, but you might still be buzzing and eager to see more clients. Once again I remind you to review all the steps outlined in this book, especially the coming chapters about mentoring, paperwork, goal setting and expanding your product range. If you have energy, feel good, want to keep the growth happening, and your personal life is in balance, then your lull is the perfect time to research what else needs to be done and what else is possible.

Most of all, do not allow yourself to believe that the lull is permanent because if you persevere, stay positive, get your life back in balance, double check that you have done and are doing all you can, then the lull will end and you will be busy again soon. There was a time that having one client could make the difference for me between paying my rent or not — and I mean my rent at home not just at my practice! There were times when kind friends bailed me out and family members loaned me money so that I could keep going. It was tough and I hope you never have to go through that, but I kept my attitude positive and kept going, whilst working part time and doing whatever I could do to prop up my finances.

The final step about planning for the lull is extremely important. No one told me about this step in advance so I had to find out about it myself, the hard way. Planning ahead has to become one of your habits if you want your practice to succeed. The time to start is now, before you have even had a lull. One of the key aspects of business that new business people ignore is the need to have some money in the bank. Seems obvious doesn't it? But so often in my work I hear people complain about their 9 to 5 jobs and their part-time work because they are so hungry for that change and the life of working as a practitioner. If you don't retain anything else from this book you will have learned a lot if you only retain this. Do not throw away your regular income until you are absolutely sure that you can manage on what you earn from your practice. That's it. That's the most important thing you need to absorb, nothing gets you through a lull more painlessly than having a bit of money to fall back on and/or a part-time job where you can increase your hours, now and then, when you need to.

When employed people say to me "I just want to leave my job. I can't stand it any more. The vibe at the office is so negative!" I suggest to them that they look upon that job as a valuable asset that is a means to an end, and start saving every penny they can for the day they do leave, because they are going to need it.

There is another form of planning that is crucial to your long-term success and to getting you and your practice through a lull — planning ahead. Lulls can happen for a lot of reasons and they aren't always within your control. Reasons such as economic downturns, a change of receptionist, other practitioners or management at your professional centre, personal issues, weather events and so on. If you are thinking and planning ahead you at least have plans in place that can stimulate your business and help to keep you feeling engaged and positive. Thinking and planning ahead is a very important habit to cultivate and needs to become part of your DNA as a practitioner.

A simple example from my own life revolves around the seasons and school holidays here in Australia. December and January are summer in Australia and also encompass the longest school break of the year. So I know that those two months will be the quietest for me. I plan for this by locking in events that will take place in February and March and I start promoting them in October or November so that I can generate revenue from them through bookings and deposits. I also plan ahead for the Christmas period by promoting special offers and gift vouchers for Christmas gifts, again starting in September or October. This planning, combined with the smaller number of people who come to me for readings during that period, is enough to keep my business humming along, but I need to start promoting the February and March events in October and November because if I left it all until after the school break finished at the end of January it would be too little too late and they would never happen, thus wasting the first three months of the year.

In order for me to run courses and workshops in February and March I actually need to book the venue first and be clear about the content of what I am going to present. That process usually starts about six months before the course or workshop actually takes place, back in July. Are you starting to see the pattern here? I'm always planning ahead, and I look at my practice from an annual perspective that includes a lull or two that I can look forward to, such as summer on the beach in Australia, while knowing I have done all I can to get the new year off to a flying start in February. If you are in the northern hemisphere you can simply swap the months around and make sure you have plenty planned. You will clarify your ideas and book the venues around March/April and begin promoting them in May and June so that when they take place in September and October you'll enjoy the success.

Lulls in your own country and region can also be balanced out by the busy times in other parts of the world. For example, when it's summer break here in Australia my clients in the USA, UK and Europe are in the depths of their winter. It's a great time for them to have a private reading, check out my blog or do my online course. So utilise the global market place if you want to keep yourself busy and your practice consistent.

In the early days of my practice, long before I had the courage to host workshops or write books, I still applied this forward planning to the annual events local to me — from the seasons, school holidays and public holidays right through to the big local festivals and smaller events organised by local groups I attended. I planned special promotions for Mother's Day, Father's Day, Christmas, Easter and school holidays, and promoted them well ahead of time so the lulls that still occurred didn't hit me so hard. It's actually very exciting to get your creative juices flowing and keep planning promotions and events six to twelve months ahead. If the professional centre you work from doesn't have an annual open day then you can suggest one, and then plan to present and promote yourself there while helping to organise the event as well.

There are so many ways you can keep your business growing. So take advantage of the occasional lull to catch up with friends, spend time with family, re-energise your hobbies or just put your feet up and relax.

Goal setting and administration

Paperwork and administration are very low on my list of exciting things to do, but like it or not it's part of running my practice. I do the basics and then hand my paperwork over to my accountant on an annual basis. So I am not going to spend a whole chapter talking about how I file my receipts. The admin part of this chapter is about motivating you to keep at least some semblance of order in your paperwork because it will benefit you in the long run.

Many people who have never run their own business before are not aware of all the expenses they can claim. This is definitely worth looking into because it can save you money at tax time and help you justify legitimate purchases for your business. It's worth having a monthly envelope or folder system for all your receipts and invoices, keeping a book where you record them by hand or using a spreadsheet or accounting program. Your willingness to spend the time and money with a bookkeeper and/or accountant, in the early days of your practice, will be a worthwhile investment. Just one appointment can take a lot of the mystery and confusion out of what is expected of you as a business person and what claims you can make on your business expenses.

I sometimes laugh when people tell me how lucky I am to be able to claim much of my travel as a business expense. Sure, I claim what I can but the fact is I have to pay for those costs first! Being able to claim certain costs on your business doesn't mean you suddenly start travelling first class. Different rules, regulations and laws apply in each state and country. It is your responsibility to find out where you stand. Once you have registered your business name and have the corresponding registration number, you are set to go.

If you are working from home you may now be entitled to claim a percentage of your rent, electricity, gas, cleaning and other running costs associated with keeping that space operational as your business premises. Even simple things like tissues, candles, massage oils, towels, music, flowers and magazines for your reception area, may also be valid expenses. If you make your clients a cup of tea or coffee on arrival then claim the costs associated with that. It's all coming out of your pocket so don't just wave it away as trivial. You work hard for what you earn and these expenses can really add up over a year. It can also be worth keeping a logbook for your car as it may surprise you when you add up the work-related miles you are driving each week. In many states and countries you are only required to keep your logbook for six months. So check with your accountant about the minimum time required wherever your business is registered.

Another important expense you can potentially claim, is your ongoing professional development. If I attend a retreat as a student, purchase a tutorial online or meet with a mentor, I claim them as expenses for keeping my business and myself healthy, balanced and current. All the courses you are required to attend to stay registered and accredited in your field, and all the conferences you attend, are part of creating and maintaining a successful practice.

If you already write, or plan to, think about the travel and research you need to do in order to write authentically. One of my upcoming projects is a set of oracle cards based on the wisdom and history of South and Central America. I cannot write authentically about these lands, peoples, cultures and their practices without travelling in these regions myself. I have already been to Mexico, Peru, Bolivia, Chile and Argentina once, and plan to go again soon to continue deepening my knowledge, meeting with local people and taking photographs. All of which will be used directly and indirectly in the creation of these cards. I'm also passionate about the Spanish language and have given readings, and even a workshop, in Argentina. So when I went to Mexico in 2014, I attended a language school for two weeks as part of my vision of having a bilingual practice.

My accountant always asks me to clarify where I travelled to and how much of it was work related. I keep all receipts and do the currency conversions as well. It's a bit of an effort, but it's much better than spending thousands of dollars and not being able to claim the business related costs, such as a portion of the flights and accommodation. If you already have some skill in a second language I highly recommend that you develop that language to a professional level. It's a joy to be able to communicate with people in more than one language and it will open up a whole new market for you. We all know that China and India are boom markets, but don't overlook fascinating countries like the Czech Republic where, after decades of communist rule, they are now hungry for what we take for granted in the West.

So what has boring old admin got to do with goal setting? Goal setting should be exciting and something you want to do regularly right? Well, I have put it in this chapter because it should be a regular part of your business routine, just like staying on top of your paperwork. When it comes to goal setting I've seen too many people treat their practice like a 'set and forget' project, or they think goal setting is akin to daydreaming about what you would like to happen. If, however, you learn to take a regular and methodical approach to your goal setting then you will magically find that many of them actually come to fruition, with few challenges along the way. My angels and guides use an interesting metaphor here. They say, 'Think of yourself sailing a yacht across a great ocean from one country to another. There are islands, reefs and currents along the way, plus some changes in the weather that may not be easy to predict. If you simply set your course on departure and never consult your charts and instruments again, you will not reach your destination and will most likely wind up shipwrecked.

If you check your charts regularly, reset and adjust your course in harmony with the conditions, and remain engaged, not only will you reach your destination, you will be much more likely to enjoy the journey as well.'

Setting goals regularly is a form of positive visualisation, a manifestation, and simply makes good business sense. As you begin to think about and clarify your goals, it will become clearer to you what actions you need to take in order to attain them. Setting goals will help you to become more skilled in establishing lead times for your promotions and events and will make you feel like the captain of your ship, rather than a stowaway down there with the luggage. Your goals must always incorporate some flexibility, not just because something 'bad' might happen but also because flexibility allows you to expand, diversify and go where the doors want to open.

A great way to get a handle on your goals and wrestle them into a format you can comprehend and work with, is to get a whiteboard that complements your handwritten or electronic journal. I begin by writing my weekly, monthly, yearly, three-year and five-year goals in my journal, first. Then, I create a kind of flow chart for the coming year so I can see where and when I will be doing readings, holding a workshop or whatever. Your goals also need to include all the fundamentals such as how many clients you want to be seeing by the middle of the year, and then by the end of the year. Your list of goals is not just a fantasy wish list. It's a clarification of what you want in the short-to-medium term future, which will motivate you.

Here is what your goals might look like if you have just graduated or just established your new practice :

Weekly goals —
- I would like to be seeing a minimum of two paying clients each week and practise on at least two friends or family members for free, for the next three months.

Three-month goals —
- at the end of three months I will cease offering free treatments and see only paying clients.
- within three months I would like to be practising one day a week at a professional centre.
- I will have a website.

Six-month goals —
- as I approach six months of practice I would like to be seeing at least four to six paying clients per week, between my home and professional practice.
- I will put promotions in place for upcoming holidays — Easter, Mother's day, Father's day, 4th of July celebrations, Thanksgiving (or whatever events are coming up in this time).
- I will take a stand at a one-off festival or fair so I can get a feeling for promoting myself at such events.

If it works I'll book another one for later in the year.

Twelve-month goals —
- by the end of this year I would like to be seeing at least eight paying clients per week.
- at least two months before Christmas I will offer a small range of books and oracle cards to sell to my clients.
- I will have added a shop page to my website so people can buy these new products from me online.

A list of goals such as this is simple, comprehensive and clear. It relates instantly to your year planner or whiteboard flow chart because it becomes obvious that, in order to achieve most of your goals, you will need to get into action weeks or months beforehand. And yes, it relates back to your financial administration efforts too, because if you are keeping track of your earnings and expenses you will soon notice when and where you need to increase your earnings or decrease your expenses. They all dovetail in together, making your practice a living entity that is more than the sum of its parts, rather than just something you do.

The other interesting realisation you may have from your goal-setting process, is the way in which you will need to work with other people. You'll have to make enquiries, hire professionals, book venues, make appointments in advance and count on these other people to do their part well. So your own organisation and communication skills will sometimes be put to the test, which again can bring us back to admin. If you don't keep clear records of the enquiries you make, their responses, your bookings, orders and other commitments, you could end up in a muddle. It's not difficult or complicated. You just need to be consistent. The most important person in your practice is you. Your colleagues, clients and suppliers will care, to a point, but the buck will stop with you every time. So regularly checking in with your emails, bank statements, credit card statements, diary and whiteboard, will help you stay balanced.

Like a character in a book, your business will begin to take on a life of its own with its own rhythms, needs, good points and downsides. Looking at your business this way helps you keep it in perspective too. Remember, you want to own and run your practice, not the other way around. Another one of my favourite sayings, and an attitude I live my life by, is 'Have faith and tie up your camel'. It's a quirky saying with its origins in Arabic culture. It means that I 'have faith'; I trust my intuition, go where the doors open, meditate regularly and ask my angels and guides for help every day, and I also 'tie up my camel', which means that I still do all my admin and goal setting to the best of my ability.

I don't live in faerie land and I don't live in my head. Years of growing my practice, working with people, learning to keep myself healthy and balanced and following my dreams, has taught me that a blend of trust and practicality is essential. So I cheer you along as you walk your path with heart, while at the same time urging you to keep tabs on the details so that camel of yours doesn't run away.

CHAPTER FIFTEEN

THE VALUE OF MENTORING

One of my favourite phrases is 'You don't know what you don't know'. Just think about this for a moment. You know what you know. For example, I know that I can drive a car, see angels and spirit guides and speak reasonable Spanish. You know what you don't know. For example, I know that I cannot fly an airplane, write computing software or speak Mandarin, but you don't know what you don't know. So what does this mean? For me, I find this an exciting and humbling way of looking at life. Acknowledging that I don't know what I don't know means that there is a Universe of possibility out there that hasn't yet shown itself to me. It's also a tad daunting because of the way our monkey minds handle this aspect of human life — assuming that everything we know and don't know is related purely to what we can see — which leaves us vulnerable to events and outcomes we didn't know we didn't know about!

'You don't know what you don't know' is one of the main reasons I am writing this book, because time and again I have seen graduates follow the monkey-mind road, based on assumptions, and wind up in uncomfortable dead ends. Heaven knows I have done this myself often enough because I had no clue what questions to ask in the first place. How can you get the support and advice you need if you don't even know what questions to ask? The ramifications of not knowing what you don't know, and therefore not knowing what questions to ask, can be painful and show up frequently in areas of practice such as starting at a professional centre or setting up your website. Mistakes are understandable because you really didn't know, but you are the one who will be left to deal with the domino effect from the questions you never thought to ask.

Mentoring therefore is vital, and I don't mean the kind of 'mentoring' you get from people at the same level as you. Your fellow students are smart and well-meaning people, but if they have never run a holistic health practice of their own before, then they are not in a position to give you the guidance you need.

The great danger in our quick-fix, instant gratification, online culture is that you will be indoctrinated with the idea that everything is supposed to be quick and simple. Some things are, but the majority are not. So unless you are a marketing, computing, internet, website, graphic design and financial whiz kid, on top of being confident in the skills recently acquired in your new modality, you are going to need some support. Humility and the willingness to seek out, and pay for, support from an experienced and successful professional will prove to be amongst your greatest assets.

Yes, engaging a mentor can seem expensive and your monkey mind will enjoy taunting you with constant doubts about how you could have spent the money elsewhere and how creating a successful practice really isn't all that difficult. Please ignore these monkey-mind, ego-based beliefs that tell you that you should know how to do this all yourself, because they are hogwash. They are a complete and utter delusion that refuses to acknowledge that you don't know what you don't know. If running a successful small business was easy, everyone would be doing it. Many people try and most of them fail within two years. You do not want to become part of that statistic.

Mentoring can come in a variety of forms. If your budget is tight then please explore what is being offered by your local council, community groups, government and colleges. Go and comb your bookstore for books that cover good business practice in general, and apply the guidelines from these books to your specific circumstances. You can also look for online tutorials, as long as you bear in mind that you cannot always verify the credentials, experience and success levels of online mentors and coaches.

The college you studied with may offer mentoring in some form, and check with some of your lecturers, if they haven't already offered mentoring. I also offer a mentoring program, which is another option you might like to consider. My Professional Supervision Program is specifically tailored to your needs and current situation. In practical terms, it consists of two thirty-minute calls per month for the duration you choose — usually three, six or twelve months. Calls are done via Skype, FaceTime, WhatsApp or telephone wherever you are in the world. So if you are enjoying this book and finding it helpful, you can take your journey to a whole new level by working with me in person. Please see the 'Intuitive Spiritual Mentoring & Coaching Programs' page on my website for more information. www.belindagrace.com

So rather than looking upon mentoring as an expense you don't need during the costly process of establishing your practice, I would encourage you to look upon it as a basic necessity that will save you time, money and angst. One unnecessary dead end can take days, weeks or even months to find your way out of, and when you are in small business, time is definitely money. So be honest with yourself and look at the bigger picture of long-term stability and success. A good mentor will recognise what you don't know and be able to reveal those vital areas to you, thus opening up new worlds of awareness and understanding. This new awareness will bring you a huge sense of relief and a greater sense of empowerment, as you learn about the questions you need to ask and have your experienced successful mentor to return to for feedback.

Any prospective mentor should be willing to share their story with you before you commit to paying them for their services. So if this information isn't clearly laid out on their website, here are some good questions to ask. They may well direct you to specific pages of their website in response to your questions, so don't be put off by that; a good mentor is busy and in demand, so if the information is already available they won't want to write it all out again. Do your research thoroughly too, by reading the 'About' and 'Testimonials' pages on their website, browsing their Facebook pages, reading their blog and signing up for their newsletter so you can get a good feeling for what they offer.

How long have you been in practice for?

Where have you practised in the past and where are you practising now?

Is your work as a practitioner your main source of income? This question is not about prying into their income. It is about understanding their situation and how crucial the success of their practice is to their overall lifestyle.

Can you provide me with at least three testimonials from people who have undertaken mentoring with you in the last five years?

Once you have read up as much as you can about your prospective mentor and contacted them with these questions, when necessary, your final arbiter must be your own intuition. If working with this person, group or organisation feels right to you then you will learn something and benefit. Try to remember that mentors are only human too and that being mentored does not relieve you of your responsibility for your own choices and actions. Even if a mentor urges you to do x rather than y, you are still the one who has to choose and live with the outcomes. A good mentor will help you to step beyond your comfort zone and give you plenty of encouragement, but they should never insist that you do or try something you are not comfortable with. They should never bully or belittle you or act disappointed if you didn't follow their advice.

Even if it takes you three times longer to accomplish something that they believe you should accomplish, it's your life, your journey and your practice. A good mentor needs to be able to walk that fine line between prodding you along the road of growth and success, while working with you at a pace you can manage. This is often very difficult for the mentor, and it can take time for the mentor to fully understand the client's situation, personality and business style. So it's important to remember that mentoring is an interactive partnership. The more open and honest you are with your mentor, the more they will be able to guide and assist you.

Every good mentor should hold you to account, set time parameters for specific tasks and be prepared to refer you to experts in other fields that they are not experienced in themselves. If any advice a mentor gives you deviates wildly from other advice you have been given, or encountered elsewhere, it's important to ask them to clearly outline why their approach is so different and request evidence of its necessity and success.

Before embarking on a mentoring program, even if you only intend to have one or two meetings, do everything you can to clarify your goals and specify what you would like your program to assist you with. You'll need to be realistic about how much can be achieved in the amount of time you'll be spending with your mentor, and this is another area in which the mentor can give you some guidelines. Managing expectations is one of the most difficult aspects of mentoring because some clients really do believe that they only need to learn a few 'tricks of the trade' to become successful. This is simply not the case, and a superficial approach such as this will not create a successful practice. The best approach you can take to mentoring is to be responsible for your own preparation, goal setting and list of questions. Then, you must also be responsible for being open and honest with your mentor and be willing to follow through and complete the actions required to move your practice forward. Ask all the questions that your time together allows and be open to the miracle of discovering what you didn't know you didn't know, and numerous new doors will open.

CHAPTER SIXTEEN

VARIETY IS THE SPICE OF LIFE

One of the challenges inherent in most jobs and many businesses is the limit placed upon your earnings potential when you are solely exchanging your time for money. This means that you can never earn more than the number of consultations you can offer in a week, multiplied by how much you charge for those consultations. So the only way to increase your income is to develop a range of add-ons and other products or services. Look around you at how other industries do this. Airline companies that charge more for checked luggage or priority seating. Hotels offer room service, movie rentals or luxury spa treatments. Museums and art galleries offer a voucher for their restaurant or café, on entry. Everywhere you look you will see that add-ons and affiliate marketing are adding to the bottom line of many successful businesses.

But you are just one person, right? A sole practitioner with very little capital to spare, so what additional income streams could you create now that your practice is busier, and you have the basics established? Well, there are endless possibilities, limited only by your imagination and willingness to try them. In this age of internet shopping, you could find that you have a global market for your lavender-filled sleep pillows, chemical-free skin cleanser, e-cookbook full of great vegan recipes and colourful pictures, or recorded guided meditations. A little creativity could see you earning money while you sleep, which is a great feeling and excellent for your bank balance.

You can also generate a healthy income stream by selling existing products that complement your work, such as crystals, essential oils, supplements, massage mitts, yoga mats, clothing, books, candles, crystal salt lamps, incense, skin care products, dietary aides, detox kits, jewelry, oracle card decks, event tickets, hair accessories, ear candling kits, meditation stools and so on. The list goes on and on. If you discover a product you love using yourself, then enquire about becoming a distributor. If networking is your thing you could consider signing up with a network marketing company so you can sell their product through your practice and also make a percentage of sales from the people who sign up under you. Please note that I am not recommending network marketing per se, personally it is not a system that appeals to me, but I have seen other practitioners do very well with health-related product ranges.

You may wish to create some affiliate programs, with stores and providers at the professional centre you work in, local businesses and/or online. If there is a great whole foods and supplement store in your area why not speak to the manager about how you can generate business for one another. This will give you both the opportunity to promote your businesses and create more sales. Your clients will appreciate it too, as long as you choose quality affiliations.

Creating and branding your own small product range is an excellent idea. Remember the 80/20 rule? Twenty per cent of your clients will give you eighty per cent of your business if you provide them with great service and a product range that relates well to, and complements, the treatments you offer in your consultations. It is so much easier, and usually more profitable, to work with return clients and make add-on sales to existing clients, than it is to constantly have to attract new clients. Once people trust you there is a golden opportunity to offer them more. So please don't let that opportunity slip away. Even to this day I love it when someone buys one of my books or oracle card decks at the end of their consultation. It's a thrill for me because I am proud of my work, I know that it will be helpful for them and it's extra income that I didn't have to put any extra time into earning. Yes it took me considerable time to write my books and cards, but once a quality product is created it will bless you with added income for many years to come.

One of my graduates holds a stand once a month at his local market. It's an outdoor Sunday market with a strong focus on health and spirituality. He and his partner don't do readings on the stand but they promote the readings they do at a local professional centre and also promote the events they host at the healing- and workshop rooms they have set up in their home. Whenever I am in town I do readings and offer workshops at their home, from which they take a percentage. So not only am I helping to bring more people to their business by publicising my events and readings there, they are also generating more income by hosting me, and people like me, who are looking for venues. At the monthly market they sell books and card decks by me and other authors, as well as salt lamps, incense and candles. It's great networking for their practice and good cash business on market days.

After you have been in practice for a few years and have the relevant experience to back them up, another wonderful way to leverage your time is to offer courses and workshops, both in person and online. There is no limit to the kind of courses and workshops you can create once you have confidence in your work, plenty of great case studies to refer back to, and an awareness of what your client base is looking for. Another of my graduates used to be a preschool teacher and has a lovely affinity with children. So he asked me if he could tailor one of my workshops to the mother and child market. He had completed my five-day residential course, both as a student and then again as a trainee teacher. So he already had my permission to present some of my material to adult audiences. We then collaborated on rewriting the course for youngsters and it's been a satisfying success. So if you see a niche market available to you based on the training you already have, why not contact your educators and suggest your own developments of their material.

Naturally you can create your own courses and programs from scratch. This takes time, dedication and a willingness to put yourself out there, and it can be enormously rewarding. Personally, I really enjoy having variety in my work, and I know I wouldn't be happy if I only had one-to-one consultations all the time. I love working with groups, enjoy public speaking and relish the one-day residential intensive courses, for the opportunity I get to spend more time with my students. Offering courses and workshops is great for your bottom line because you can offer the course at an affordable price to the individual while increasing your earning power by working with a group, rather than one person at a time. Then, if you sell physical products like books, cards, oils and candles you can sell them at the workshop or include them in an early-bird package as an incentive to people to book before a certain date.

Your courses and workshops must have substance and be based on experience. All too often I see people who have only been practising for a short time, setting out to offer a workshop and wanting to 'teach'. Before you busy yourself teaching others please make sure that you have some considerable experience yourself and understand that just because someone has enrolled in your workshop it doesn't mean that they are going to be open and receptive.

Over the years, I have had plenty of sceptical, nervous, desperate and closed people come to my workshops and courses. They are all looking for something. So I have huge respect for them based on the fact that they have made the effort to come along, but they aren't always easy to deal with. You need to gain experience in dealing with sceptics, needy people who would hijack the whole workshop for their own questions, and people who have intense reactions. At one workshop, years ago, a woman fainted and fell off her chair. At another big one-day event a woman spontaneously stood up while I was talking and sang a loud, clear note that went on for about thirty seconds! While she sang out I asked my Guidance what the heck was going on, and they told me that Archangel Michael was communicating through her. The story is longer than that, but I took hold of the situation, reassured the 150-plus audience and had a fascinating conversation with the songbird during the lunch break. You really do have to be prepared for anything.

If you waffle and waste time, let members of the audience dominate with their own agendas, or become anxious when someone challenges you, then the course or workshop will most likely be a flop. My suggestion is to start with something very simple and build up your content from there. About fifteen years ago I started by offering basic workshops about chakra balancing. The workshop only lasted for two hours and I only took a maximum of eight people. They loved it, asked me to run more complex workshops and I learned a great deal about how to handle groups, group dynamics and the needs and demands of all concerned. Even to this day, I still only accept a maximum of eight people into each five-day residential course, in order to give each person plenty of time and attention, while caring for my own needs and energy levels.

A note about public speaking — I am aware that many people feel terrified by the prospect of speaking in front of a group, but it is such a joy once you have built your confidence. There are some excellent courses available in public speaking in general, and presentation skills for business, specifically. One of the most well known organisations worldwide is

Toastmasters. Take a look at their website for your local group. Back when I was in high school, around age seventeen, I did a course with Toastmasters, which is something I have always been grateful for having the chance to participate in.

The online world can also offer you immense opportunities for additional income streams that will expand your practice. You can create online courses that are ready made and that download in one go, or over a period of time. You can offer live webinars through platforms such as Zoom and Google Hangouts. You can create a series that people subscribe to, and if you are talented in that way maybe you can even compose music that clients can pay for and download. For example, one of my graduates plays the harp and works specifically with people in crisis, even travelling to see them at home and in hospital. So I am encouraging her to record and reproduce her work for broader audiences, so she can have another income stream from her gifts.

Take your time getting to know your client base and the kind of add-on purchases they might prefer. Ask them what else they are looking for when they come to see someone with your skills. Make enquiries as to what else would interest or help them. Remember to start small and work your way up. When ordering stock of any kind, such as books or essential oils, always order the minimum amount and never just order the items you like most. You need to start with a broad range, more variety and less depth, at first, so that you can discover what your clients really want.

All in all you can discover and create many ways to keep your practice fresh, add interest for yourself and your clients, and increase your earnings by going beyond the one-to-one consultation. For me individual consultations are the basis of everything else I do. This is where I learn most about my clients' needs and attitudes. It's where I gain a great deal of my experience, and then these clients create the foundation from which I grow my business, as they move on to my books, oracle cards, workshops, courses and online material. It's a wonderful mix and keeps me engaged and excited every single day. So keep note of your ideas, your clients' comments and requests, market trends and your own preferences. Review all of these regularly until your new business opportunity comes into clear focus. Then reach for the stars while keeping your feet firmly planted on the ground in commercial, daily reality.

CHAPTER SEVENTEEN

SUCCESSFUL IS AS SUCCESSFUL DOES

Establishing and maintaining a practice in the holistic health and healing field requires a huge amount of energy and commitment. So it is very important to acknowledge your successes and achievements along the way. The small victories that don't appear to be life changing at first are often the ones that will have greater impact in the long term. Acknowledging your small successes will feed positive energy into them and ensure that you attract more of the same, and you will learn something valuable from each experience.

There are many definitions of success out there and most of them seem to revolve around being wealthy and popular. There is nothing wrong with wealth or popularity if that's what you want, and financial security is essential to doing your work well. But there are so many other forms of success that are overlooked in that one dimensional 'rich + famous = success' equation.

Success is about discovering who you are, what you are capable of, overcoming your own doubts and fears, improving yourself, stepping outside your comfort zone, creating a unique lifestyle, being your own boss, having the freedom to be creative, living with courage, trusting your intuition and your gut feelings, supporting yourself, creating something original, inspiring yourself and others, feeling excited about each day, setting healthy boundaries, feeling valued for who you are, and standing for something you believe in. The list of real and meaningful successes is truly endless.

I believe that the world would be a better place if everyone had to run their own business at some point in their lives. When your wellbeing depends on what you are able to create, attract and generate, and the buck stops with you every time, concepts such as value for money, clear communication and responsibility take on a whole new level of meaning. You realise that nothing comes for free, and you also realise, quite paradoxically, that when you put your heart and soul into something that's important to you the Universe will support you in the most miraculous of ways. So the most important thing you need to prepare for, is success.

It's ironic that so many practitioners and small-business people put so much effort into delivering their best without ever consciously preparing for success. They usually want to succeed but are often unprepared for it. Acknowledging your small successes along the way helps you to become accustomed to the greater success you are creating across the entirety of your life. Every time you say to yourself '*Wow this worked. I did it!*' you are looking at yourself in a new light and learning to be comfortable with turning your ideas and efforts into positive outcomes. Successes achieved when you are employed by someone else are wonderful, but they are just not the same as your first paying client, your first website, your first online sale, your first day at a professional centre, and so on, because you made all of those things happen.

So congratulations, you are a success because you have already displayed immense commitment, courage and passion in order to come this far. In life, we can always look further along the road and see that there is still a long way to go. This is a good thing, otherwise we would become bored and complacent. So don't be disheartened by this distant view. Every journey has lookouts, rest points, plateaus and detours. There is no perfect road that you can simply find to cruise along without a hitch, there is only your road with its many unique features, attractions and successes along the way.

Finding the discipline and motivation to do what is necessary each day is a massive part of your already successful life. You are not the norm and you are not average. You haven't just sat around talking about what you might do one day. You are doing it, and you are living it. At times, it is so easy to get caught up in your 'to do' list that the only thing that seems to matter is getting everything done and crossing them off. Well, as you and I both know, whenever we cross something off that list we find something else to add. It's endless, so you need to stop and enjoy your successes and victories as they happen, otherwise all you'll ever think about is what's next on the list.

So this chapter is about savouring this moment, no matter where you are at today. Maybe you have not yet completed your studies, so celebrate the progress you have made thus far and recommit to finishing and getting your diploma or degree. Maybe you have recently graduated and are feeling a little overwhelmed by the options. Make sure you deeply acknowledge yourself for completing your studies, which is a huge accomplishment at any age. You've done it! And now you have a new array of opportunities before you. Maybe you have worked with a few well-meaning friends, but no paying clients have booked yet. That's great! You are gaining experience and developing your confidence. Celebrate the fact that you have already shared your skills with other people. Maybe you are only seeing paying clients now and are wishing you had a whole lot more. How amazing you are! Look at what you have achieved in such a short space of time. Notice how your friends admire you and want to encourage you. Notice how the people around you react. Notice who you have become.

After the key step of acknowledging your successes, big and small, the other vital step is to be grateful for where you are at right now. Happiness rarely turns out to be what we think it is or what we expect. Happiness is usually a great deal more subtle. There are still days when I charge through my 'To do' list as if the sky would fall in on my head if I didn't get all those tasks done. I guess the difference for me now, compared to when I started out twenty years ago, is that I am owning my successes and enjoying them.

There are plenty of clairvoyants out there who do more readings than me and authors who have sold more books. We can always find someone to compare ourselves to and find ourselves wanting, but that's not how I look at my life. For me happiness comes from being who I am, not trying to be something or someone else. It comes from being content with what I have achieved, while knowing that the possibilities for more growth are still endless.

By all means, learn from others who appear to be more successful than you currently are. Harness their success as motivation for your own upward journey, but don't ever compare yourself with others, because it is fruitless and pointless. You are a unique person and so are they. You can never fully know what has challenged and motivated them, inspired and informed them, driven them to despair and brought them joy. You can learn a great deal from other people but you cannot *be* them. You can only be your true, authentic self. So prepare to succeed in your own unique way. Use this book to help you create a framework, good habits and structure, like scaffolding around a building, and then design your own Shangri-La.

CHAPTER EIGHTEEN

THE FUTURE LOOKS BRIGHT

Holistic health and healing is a growth industry with more and more people looking for natural, sustainable and non-invasive approaches to their health and happiness, every day. Many people are seeking greater meaning, a deeper sense of satisfaction, higher awareness, and answers to questions that a purely materialistic approach to health and happiness cannot answer. So as practitioners in this field we have a bright future and a great deal to look forward to.

Through your practice you can have an enormously positive impact on the lives of other people, which means that you will ultimately have an enormously positive impact on the world. For each person you connect with, they will go out and connect with hundreds of others. This is not about whether they recommend your services to other people or not. This is about the positive energy they will naturally share with others after a consultation with you. When we feel well, calm, healthy, energised, balanced, informed and empowered, we share that higher vibration with other people, just by showing up. So when a stressed, unhealthy client comes to see you and you send them home feeling lighter and more positive, with tools to care better for their own health, you are sending them back to their friends and families as unwitting healers. What you do and what you offer can, and will, make a difference.

There is an increasing understanding in the wider community that many health challenges will not respond well to drugs or surgery. There is an increasing willingness to discover the root causes of every disease, from depression to diabetes. So in this role you also become an educator, a door opener and a bridge builder for all these people seeking alternatives to the mainstream view. There are well over seven billion people on this planet and all of them, at some point in their lives, will experience loss, grief, illness and a desire to create some sense of meaning in their lives beyond going to work and paying the mortgage.

The future looks bright because the number of people who genuinely want to heal, to be truly well and be more involved in their own health, is growing. You have chosen to be part of this paradigm shift and to make your contribution. That's wonderful and it's something to be proud of. You have chosen to dedicate a large amount of your energy and time to being your best and sharing that with others. So when you are consulting with a client who feels lost, whose situation is difficult or daunting, don't be afraid to share your own personal story with them. They will be inspired by your determination and strength. They will realise that your life wasn't handed to you on a plate, and they will realise that they can do it too.

The future looks bright because we all have the chance to recover from our illnesses. We all have the chance to improve our health. We all have the chance to make a contribution. We all have the chance to be uniquely successful. We all have the chance to thrive rather than merely survive. We all have the chance to let go of the baggage that is weighing us down. We all have the chance to inspire others We all have the chance to create and find deeper meaning. We all have the chance to attain higher levels of awareness, and we all have the chance to become enlightened.

As a practitioner in the holistic health and healing field you have the chance, every day and with every client, to be a mentor and a guide as well. You have this chance, this privilege, to share small portions of the lives and journeys of others, with them.

The future is looking bright because everyone is looking for these things, and you will be there to support them.

Namasté, BelindaGrace

True Love Reading Cards
Attract and Create the Love You Desire
Illustrations by Lori Banks

Discover your true pathway to love! Do you have questions about romance, relationships and love? Would you like to meet that special someone or bring the joy back into your current relationship? These cards have been created to guide you in matters of the heart.

• 96 pp. 36 cards • Magnetic close box
• 978-1-925017-41-0

Clairvoyant Reading Cards
Illustrations by Elaine Marson

This true oracle will take you by the hand and will show you how to develop your strengths, explore forgotten areas of your inner world and encourage you to trust your own intuition, clairvoyance and Divine Guidance more and more.

• 96 pp. 36 cards • Magnetic close box
• 978-1-925017-42-7

Available at all good book stores or online at
www.rockpoolpublishing.com.au

Other products by BelindaGrace

You Are Abundant
Why You Are Enough the Way You Are

In today's fast-paced world many people crave what they think they need a bigger house, a newer car, yet more clothes, a better body and worry about how to get it. They fear they lack the abundance required to make their lives happy. This book defines a new form of abundance that is essential to happiness, healing and a sense of purpose in life.

• 210mm x 135mm • 256 pp. Paperback •
978-1-921878-59-6

You Are Inspired
An Intuitive Guide to Life with
Meaning & Purpose

Filled with inspiring true stories, easy to follow exercises, You are Inspired will help you make the transition to the inspiring life you know you can live.

•210mm x 135mm • 288 pp. Paperback
978-1-921295-23-2

Heaven Sent
A Simple Guide to connecting with Angels
BelindaGrace

Heaven Sent is a beautifully designed book outlining how to communicate with your angels. A perfect gift for friends in need and just to make people happy.

• 151mm x 151mm • 128 pp. Paperback
978-1-921878-02-2

Available at all good book stores or online at
www.rockpoolpublishing.com.au